Basics of Finance
for
Manufacturing Professionals

(And Those Selling to Manufacturing Companies)

An Asset Management Approach

SECOND EDITION

J. David Viale

Center for Manufacturing Education

A Financial Approach to Cost Reductions
Through the Supply-Chain

BASICS OF FINANCE FOR MANUFACTURING PROFESSIONALS

(And Those Selling to Manufacturing Companies)

An Asset Management Approach

SECOND EDITION

By J. David Viale

Center for Manufacturing Education

CREDITS

Editor: Karla A. Maree

Typesetting: Silverlining Designs

Cover Design: Daniel Burney/ideas in print

Published by CFME Press
Basics of Finance for Manufacturing Professionals
Printed in the United States of America by Publishers Press

Library of Congress Catalog Card Number 99-074777
Viale, J. David
Basics of Finance for Manufacturing Professionals
ISBN 1-928834-00-0

ABOUT THE AUTHOR

J. David Viale is the founder and president of CFME Press, and the Center for Manufacturing Education, an international training, education, and consulting company.

His background includes working for Arthur Andersen, and holding management positions at Hewlett-Packard and Fairchild Semiconductor. He was a practicing CPA and is certified in production and inventory management (CPIM).

His diverse business and teaching background gives him a unique blend of theory, application of the theory, and the financial impact. With this diverse experience, Dave brings a cross-functional perspective to his classes, speeches, seminars, and key executive presentations, which he delivers across the United States, Canada, Europe and the Far East.

Dave is the author of the APICS best-selling book, *Basics of Manufacturing*. He is also the author of *New Product Introduction, JIT Forecasting and Master Scheduling,* and *Basics of Inventory Management.* All of these books may be purchased online at www.cfme.com.

He can be contacted at:

> Phone: 408-973-0309
>
> Fax: 408-973-1592
>
> E-mail at CFME@aol.com
>
> Web Page: www.cfme.com

What's Unique About This Book?

The combination and integration of financial and manufacturing concepts makes this unique. It focuses not only on the *bottom line* but on the *top line* as well.

What's New This Second Edition?

The following items have been added to this revised edition:

- Cash-to-cash concepts and exercise (see page 69)

- What causes inventory build-up – discussion and exercise (see page 62)

- Vendor managed inventory (VMI) concepts (see page 32)

TABLE OF CONTENTS

INTRODUCTION   **vii**

CHAPTER I   **COMPETITIVE ISSUES AND THEIR IMPACT:
                  WHY ASSET MANAGEMENT?**   **1**

                  Case Study 3
                  Why Asset Management? 8
                  Handling Conflicting Objectives 14
                  Environments and Their Effects on Asset Management 15

CHAPTER II   **AN OVERVIEW OF FINANCIAL STATEMENTS
                  AND THE ROLE OF ASSET MANAGEMENT**   **21**

                  Overview of Financial Statements 23
                      The Balance Sheet 23
                      The Income Statement 26
                  Accounting Versus Finance—What's the Difference? 28
                  Categories of Hard Assets 29
                  Allocation of Factory Overhead and Activity-Based Costing 33
                  Determining Other Costs 35
                  Key Financial Ratios 38
                  The Basic Accounting/Manufacturing Formula 42
                  Forecasting Revenue 43

CHAPTER III   **TYING FINANCIAL INFORMATION TO
                  MANUFACTURING INFORMATION**   **51**

                  **Part 1: Forecasting, Master Scheduling, and Capacity
                  Management to Net Sales and A/R**

                  Manufacturing Resource Planning 53
                  Financial Impact of Insufficient Capacity 56
                  The Master Schedule 57
                  Financial Ramifications of Forecasting 61
                  Presentation A 66
                  Presentation Follow-Up 70
                  Presentation B 71

CHAPTER IV	**TYING FINANCIAL INFORMATION TO MANUFACTURING INFORMATION**	**79**

Part 2: MRP, BOM, Lead-Time, COGs, and Other Expenses

Reconciling the Physical Flow with the Financial Information Flow 81

Material Requirements Planning 82

Reducing Inventory with "Better Information" 85

Financial Impact of Customers Changing Their Mind 86

Manufacturing Resource Planning/MRPII 87

Material Requirements Planning 88

Create a Bill of Material 89

The Costed Bill of Material 91

Determine Gross-to-Net Requirements 93

CHAPTER V	**THREE CASE STUDIES**	**113**

Case Study I: What We Have Learned 115

Case Study II: Contract Terms and Conditions 122

Case Study III: Supplier with Bad Financials 125

CHAPTER VI	**FINAL PRESENTATION**	**137**

Putting It All Together 139

	PRETEST	**143**
	POST-TEST	**146**

INTRODUCTION

One of the areas frequently overlooked in the preparation of manufacturing professionals is their knowledge of business finance. While it is not necessary to master a level of detail encompassing the "accounting rules of debit and credit," it is crucial to develop an understanding of the financial ramifications and decisions made within the manufacturing environment—not only the bottom line, but the top line as well.

Employees today are often required to provide, collect, and evaluate financial data. Those in decision-making positions are expected to participate in planning and maintenance of established budgets and cost control. Promotions and raises are often assigned to individuals based on their participation in achieving departmental goals such as sales quotas, cost containment, and productivity improvements.

A basic understanding of the financial planning/implementation process, and your role within it, will help you obtain such goals. It is the aim of this book to equip you with a financial knowledge necessary for achieving the level of success that you desire in your career.

An Asset Management Approach

The approach of this book is to provide manufacturing professionals and those interfacing with manufacturing concerns (such as sales professionals) who are unfamiliar with the financial realm of business and its related concepts and terminology with invaluable cross-functional knowledge of financial-related topics and how they relate to the manufacturing environment. Specific topics include the Balance Sheet and Profit and Loss statements, key ratios such as inventory turns, return on assets (ROA) and return on investment (ROI), and the financial impact of bad forecasts, excess inventory, and customer changes. These topics are compared to their manufacturing counterparts, such as Master Scheduling, closed-loop Material Requirements Planning, and inventory management.

This book then combines the finance and manufacturing into an asset management approach, which culminates in a case study that is used to reinforce the information presented and the lessons learned.

Think of every day as a page in the resume of your life. Ask yourself, "What am I doing every day to increase my net worth, to make myself more marketable?" This book supports you in taking control of your own learning process, by continuously improving.

Pretest

In order to measure your progress and the return on your investment, turn to the pretest on page 143. At the completion of the book, take the post-test on page 146 and see how you've progressed.

> *"The Continuous Improvement Process is not only a way of doing business; it's a way of doing life—the essence of lifelong learning."*
>
> —J. David Viale

1

COMPETITIVE ISSUES AND THEIR IMPACT: WHY ASSET MANAGEMENT?

LEARNING OBJECTIVES

After completing this chapter, you will be able to:

- List the major components of the key financial statements

- Explain key terms and definitions

- Complete a financial analysis

CASE STUDY

The Asset Manager swiveled in the rather ordinary standard chair and looked out at the beautiful January weather. The Asset Manager was very pleased with the new corner office with such an expansive view.

It had been just over a year ago, before Christmas, when the Asset Manager had been parachuted in by the new CEO to take over as Vice President of Corporate Assets. The Asset Manager had mixed feelings about this "new opportunity." On the one hand, it seemed the company could use the Asset Manager's skills. On the other hand, bookings had ramped up nicely in the beginning, but then had fallen off, only to recover in the quarter just ended. However, during the prior periods, the company's assets had sky-rocketed, especially capital equipment and inventory. The accounts receivable had also shot up and collections had slowed.

One of the things that concerned the Asset Manager most was the comment that the new president, G.O. Day, had made to the Asset Manager… "These people don't have a clue – it's your job to make order out of this chaos!"

The Asset Manager was now ready to put in place a program called

> "WHAT WE HAVE LEARNED FROM OUR PAST, AND HOW WE ARE
> GOING TO PREVENT THESE MISTAKES IN THE FUTURE!"

The Asset Manager pulled out a book from the bookcase entitled *Basics of Finance for Manufacturing Professionals*. The Asset Manager intended to use this material as the basis for the training program.

Introduction

The Asset Manager had established the following objectives:

- To develop a consistent company-wide strategy that would enable the company, its customers, and suppliers, to more effectively manage assets across the entire customers–company–supplier chain.

- To develop a basic understanding of the company's key financial statements (Balance Sheet, Income Statement, and an overview of the impact of cash flowing out of and into the company).

- To develop a working knowledge of key ratios (return on assets, return on investments, inventory turns) and, as a result, implement a measurement system understood by all functional groups.

- To develop a thorough understanding of how the manufacturing systems (master scheduling, forecasting, material requirements planning [MRP], inventory management), and the decisions reflected in these systems impact the financial statements.

THE PROGRAM

The Asset Manager planned to use the following outline in order to accomplish these objectives. The idea was to present this material throughout the entire company.

Chapter I—An Overview of Competitive Issues

Chapter I provides an overview of the competitive issues facing companies today. The importance of good asset management on achieving these competitive issues is stressed.

Chapter II—An Overview of Asset Management

Chapter II provides an overview of the financial statements (Balance Sheet and Income Statement), as well as descriptions of major components of these financial statements.

Chapter III—Tying Financials to Manufacturing Information: Part I

Chapter III reinforces the key financial ratios and other financial measurements introduced in Chapter II. In this chapter, the forecasts and Master Schedule will be tied to net sales and accounts receivable.

Chapter IV—Tying Financials to Manufacturing Information: Part II

Chapter IV focuses on developing an understanding of the "tie-in" of the basic manufacturing system (Master Schedule, Forecasting, MRP, Inventory Management, and lead-time with the related financial statements, concepts, ratios, and formulas). In this session you will analyze "YOUR COMPANY'S" financial statements.

Chapter V—Case Studies

CASE STUDY I: This case study will address issues impacting net sales, accounts receivable, master scheduling, and capacity management.

CASE STUDY II: This case study will examine the impact of what happens when a contract is drawn up with unclear terms and conditions and how this affects the manufacturer and its customer.

CASE STUDY III: The emphasis in this part of the case study is on the financial ramifications of inventory and cost of goods sold. In this session, you will analyze the financial statement of a supplier.

Chapter VI—Final Presentation

The results of the program "What We Have Learned From Out Past and How We Are Going to Prevent These Mistakes In the Future!" will be summarized in a final, financial presentation.

Instructions to the Participant

You have been hired by the VP of Asset Management (the Asset Manager) to support and sell solutions to executives from different functional areas. The Asset Manager has employed you as the chief change agent. As such, you will be working along with each functional director, gathering and analyzing the data, and making recommendations and preparing a strategy that will address how the solution should be sold to the executives of the company, to customers, and to suppliers.

As you proceed through the material, you will be presented with financial statements from different types of manufacturing environments, representing your customers, your company, and your suppliers.

You will be asked to complete multiple-choice questions, do calculations, remember formulas, and develop a written presentation that will reflect your progress. These presentations will relate to lessons learned about finance and specifically asset management. These "lessons learned" will show financial ramifications of improving manufacturing processes such as forecasting, inventory management, and capacity management just to name a few.

You will take a pretest, then a post-test, to measure your progress. Your final task will be to develop a presentation in which you will pull together all of the "lessons learned." This presentation can then be reviewed with your management, peers, customers, or suppliers, depending on your individual objectives.

This material can be used individually or in a team environment.

However, as a minimum your presentation will provide a way to achieve your recommendations. The Asset Manager's objectives are stated on page 8.

If you and/or your team are successful in completing this material, you will be well on your way to more successfully managing the assets of the company.

CAST OF CHARACTERS

Before proceeding with your first assignment, take a minute and review the following notes that you made during your initial meeting with the following cast of characters.

G.O. Day	President & CEO (from Australia)
B. Burnemout (B.B.)	Vice President & General Manager
C. Countemright (C²)	Director of Finance
E.C. Oops (E.C.)	Director of R&D and Engineering
F. Fish (Fish)	Director of Marketing & Sales
F. Forecaster (F²)	Master Scheduler
E.O. Inventory (E.O.)	Director of Manufacturing

Following are the notes from your meetings.

First there was B. Burnemout, the General Manager, known for a quick aggressive style. B.B. was known for making decisions that got results, but left bodies strewn all over the place. It was "damn the torpedoes, full steam ahead"—revenues at any cost!

B.B.'s objectives were to:

- HIT THE BOTTOM LINE
- MAKE MONEY
- KEEP THE STOCK PRICES UP
- GET THE BONUS CHECK

Then there was C. Countemright, the Corporate Controller. Analytical to the hilt, C^2 was different from most accountants. As B.B. had said, "C^2 has a personality." C^2's philosophy was "numbers don't lie— You gotta hit the bottom line!"

C^2's objectives were to:

- REDUCE COSTS
- MINIMIZE INVENTORY
- IMPROVE RETURN ON ASSETS
- IMPROVE RETURN ON EQUITY
- KEEP THE STOCK PRICES UP
- GET THE BONUS CHECK

Next, there was E.C. Oops, the Director of R&D and Engineering. While noted as a "Brilliant Technical" person, it seems that during the DNA cloning process, the accuracy gene had been left out.

E.C.'s objectives were to:

- BRING PRODUCT TO MARKET FASTER AND FASTER
- STAY ON THE PROMOTIONAL FAST TRACK
- BECOME A LEGEND
- GET THE BONUS CHECK

Then there was the Director of Marketing & Sales, whose nickname was Fish. No one knew Fish's last name, or even if there was one. It was rumored that Fish was part of a witness protection program. Others said that the nickname came from the conditions of the sales forecast, while others said that Fish's forecast represented the state of the customer orders and inventory, "First-In-Still-Here."

Fish's objectives were to:

- SHIP ON TIME
- ACHIEVE CUSTOMER SATISFACTION
- MAKE QUOTA (*GET BIG COMMISSION CHECK*)
- GET THE BONUS CHECK

Then there was the Director of Manufacturing, E.O. Inventory. E.O. had been with the company from its inception.

E.O.'s objectives were to:

- GET A BIGGER WAREHOUSE FOR ALL THE INVENTORY
- SHIP ON TIME
- IMPLEMENT A SUPPLIER MANAGEMENT PROGRAM
- NEVER BACK DOWN FROM THE SALES FORECAST
- GET THE BONUS CHECK

F. Forecaster (F^2) was the next person you talked with. F^2 was known for flexibility and willingness to do "whatever" the group wanted. F^2 just didn't want problems, and said there were two types of forecast: Lucky & Lousy. That was the only lousy joke F^2 knew.

F^2's objectives were to:

- REDUCE THE FORECAST ERROR
- MAKE SURE THERE WERE NO PROBLEMS
- KEEP EVERYONE HAPPY
- ONE DAY GET PROMOTED SO F^2 COULD GET A BONUS CHECK, TOO

Finally, there was G.O. Day.

G.O.'s objectives were to:

- MEET ALL THE COMPETITIVE ISSUES
- IMPROVE THE MANAGEMENT OF ASSETS
- KEEP THE STOCK PRICES UP
- HIT THE TOP LINE AND THE BOTTOM LINE
- GET THE BONUS CHECK

WHY ASSET MANAGEMENT?

The major reason for managing assets is to address the following competitive issues, thus increasing *return on investments* (ROI) and *return on assets* (ROA).

Competitive Issues

#1 Maximizing Customer Service Through Improved Forecasting

#2 Minimizing Inventory Investment

#3 Maximizing Profit Through Cost Reductions

#4 Bringing Products to Market Faster

#5 Delivering High-Quality Products

#6 Improving Employee Training and Education

#7 Developing an Informational Organization

#8 Improving Information Exchange Systems and Networks

Now let's look at each of these in more detail. As you read through each of these potentially competitive issues, think about the issues surrounding the management of the following assets: cash, accounts receivable, inventory, machinery, equipment, and facilities. Think also about the financial impact of improperly managing these assets.

#1 Maximizing Customer Service Through Improved Forecasting

Inaccurate customer forecasts, a multitude of changes to the original customer orders, and an overall lack of account management are the major causes of poor customer service in terms of on-time delivery—the problem isn't solely with just the suppliers, nor just purchasing. The result is excessive inventory, which ultimately leads to inventory write-offs and high product cost and lower profit margins.

The more accurate the individual product-sales forecasting is, the smaller the forecast error, and the less inventory needs to be carried to maintain a specified level of customer service. By carrying less inventory, the capacity of machines required to build products is better utilized. Inventory is not built before it is needed, thus avoiding the mistake of committing capacity of machines too early. By carrying less inventory, generally less space is used, and it is not used too early.

There is a basic premise (principle) of this book that states "The larger the forecast error, the higher the desired customer service level, the more inventory that must be carried." And we are not talking about inventory at the supplier, unless there is willingness to pay expenses such as storage, insurance, and other related carrying costs. These costs are some of the major "hidden costs of manufacturing" contributing to the fact that many companies have increasing revenues and decreasing profits (and stock prices).

The solution to managing these costs is the establishment of a financial and asset management model that will be discussed throughout this book.

#2 Minimizing Inventory Investment

In manufacturing, long production runs (large lot sizes) of a single product can be more efficient than short runs. Managers are often measured by the amount of product they produce, which acts as an incentive for longer production runs. However, long runs result in inventory that sits for long periods of time. Theoretically, this inventory represents "miscommitted" capacity and a reduction in machine flexibility. Remember, if you can't ship the product relatively quickly, don't build it—no matter what the benefits of long run-time are.

Inventories tie up cash that the company could use elsewhere in the business. Excess inventory can create a negative cash flow, something that must be avoided. This is why the financial people work to keep inventories as low as possible.

#3 *Maximizing Profit Through Cost Reductions*

Increasing revenue or decreasing cost can maximize profit. One of the best ways to do this is by proper management of the company's assets.

The Power of Cost Reductions

In this example, we have:

Unit sales price:	$10.00
Profit margin percentage:	10%
Profit margin:	$1.00

If we were to decrease any cost by $1.00, the profit would double. Another way of looking at this is $1.00 in cost reduction is equal to $10 in sales.

To maximize profits, organizations need to reduce both tangible and intangible costs. This can be done by:

- Reducing the amount of time inventory spends under the company's ownership. This enables you to reduce other costs, such as rental space, insurance to cover inventory, interest on money borrowed to pay for inventory, or interest on money that could have been earned. By reducing inventory and selling it faster, you improve cash flow.

- Reducing defects and variability in the processes, such as forecast error.

- Reducing wasted time. Intangible costs might become the biggest component of getting product to the customer faster. Time is wasted by unproductive meetings, telephone tag, interruptions. More time frees you to be more productive and make more decisions.

By applying the simple techniques presented in this book, you can achieve cost reductions and improve your company's profitability.

#4 Bringing Products to Market Faster

Products are coming to market faster, and the time to recoup the investment is getting shorter because the life cycle of each succeeding product decreases. When you reduce the amount of time it takes to get each new product to market, you have less time in which to earn profit. As a result, products must be profitable sooner, so that the next generation of new products can be funded.

The typical *product life cycle* (introduction, growth, maturity, decline, and demise) shown in the illustration below demonstrates some of the issues of shorter life cycles.

A *cash cow* is a product that is beyond the break-even point and is contributing to a large portion of the company's overall profit. The *break-even* point is where revenue first equals costs.

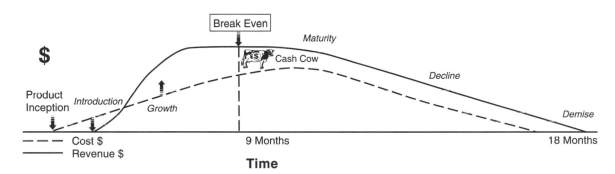

Traditional Product Life Cycle

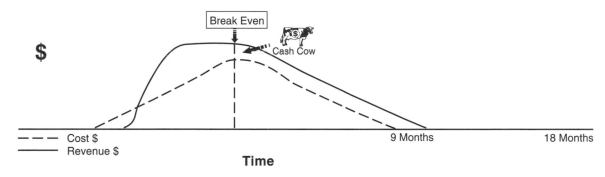

Current Product Life Cycle

#4 Bringing Products to Market Faster (continued)

The impact, if nothing is done to reduce cost significantly, is potentially devastating to the profitability over a product's lifetime. Companies are grappling with ways to change the slope of the revenue curve (up and to the left) and of the cost curve (down and to the right) by gauging success based on new measures, including:

TIME TO MARKET: How fast you can get the product to market.

TIME TO VOLUME: How fast you can produce at a volume that attracts enough revenue to cover costs.

TIME TO CONSUMPTION: How fast the customer makes the decision to buy.

TIME TO PROFIT: How fast you can generate revenue that exceeds cost.

TIME TO CHANGE: How fast you can make changes to accommodate customer requests, and how much does the change affect your profit.

TIME TO CASH: How fast you can turn shipments into accounts receivable and then into cash.

#5 Delivering High-Quality Products

Quality, and the ability to measure it, plays a crucial role in improving a company's capability to go to market faster. For companies that have been able to maintain a "quality mind-set" in their products and processes while responding to the tremendous time pressures of bringing products to market, success has been forthcoming. For those companies that have opted for the "ship-and-get-market-share-and-fix-defects-later" approach, the results have been dismal.

The key is improving quality on an ongoing basis is through the philosophy of *continuous process improvement* (CPI). CPI refers to an ongoing process that strives to identify a problem, determines its root cause, and then takes corrective action so that it doesn't happen again. When everyone is involved and processes continually improve, quality improves, costs go down, profits go up, and new products reach the market faster.

#6 Improving Employee Training and Education

People and their ability to make decisions will become a bottleneck if they lack proper training. To increase your company's ability to bring products to market faster, everyone in your company needs to be trained and educated in all facets of the business, including manufacturing and finance.

Customers will expand their purchases based not only on your products and processes, but also on your employees' education and training at all levels, including the executive levels. All too often, executives spend significant amounts of money on educating and training their employees, while neglecting their own need for remaining current. As a result, many find themselves making decisions about issues of which they have little or no understanding. The solution? Participate in the training. This is a wonderful way for them to reinforce their message and at the same time learn from their employees. Ideally, everyone in an organization should educate everyone else. Ask yourself, "What person in the organization or department would I least like our customers to talk to?" This is the person to be educated and trained first. Education and training might be the ultimate competitive weapon a company has.

#7 Developing an Informational Organization

The organizational structures within companies will have to change in order to support an increasing number of products with increasingly shorter product life cycles. Profit margins, returns on investments (ROIs) and returns on assets (ROAs) will have to be reached within increasingly shorter periods of time.

To cope with these pressures, there will be at least two organizational structures in every company:

1. The traditional *formal* organization, characterized by multiple layers of authority (including a president, other executives, and management)
2. The emerging *informational* organization

This flat organization is characterized by a less hierarchical, more team-based, decision-making environment that integrates suppliers as well as customers into an interconnected series of organizational structures, all dedicated to supporting and bringing products to market faster.

Many companies have realized that if too many people are involved in the decision-making process, the more likely it is that the product will be delayed. Within the informational organization, fewer levels of authorization are involved in the decision-making process. As a result, products come to market sooner.

#8 Improving Information Exchange Systems and Networks

Information exchange systems can also create a bottleneck. Change is happening so fast that information systems can't keep up. More advanced information exchange systems and networks must be developed to enhance the flow of information. In order to make better decisions, you need to get information faster.

The company's manufacturing systems, such as *Manufacturing Resource Planning* (MRPII) or the expanded version called *Enterprise Resource Planning* (ERP), must be integrated with the engineering design software systems, as well as sales force automation. The result will be an enormous increase in the amount of information being generated internally as well as externally by customers and suppliers alike. Needless to say, this accelerated flow of information also results in a demand to make good decisions even faster. It is possible to have a situation in the foreseeable future where data is being generated so fast that it can no longer be converted into information fast enough for individuals to make well-informed decisions, financial or otherwise. With the Internet, we might already be there. All the more reason to make sure that everyone in your company is properly trained to deal with these new realities.

HANDLING CONFLICTING OBJECTIVES

Meeting the challenges of the competitive issues just discussed requires balancing short-term as well as the long-term objectives.

When developing the business plan and functional strategies, executives must make trade-offs and decisions about such things as levels of inventory accumulation, appropriate levels of manufacturing personnel, use of part-time and temporary personnel, plant and equipment utilization, quality, outsourcing, and new-product introduction.

- The sales and marketing group attempts to balance high customer service, short, stable lead-times, broad product line, and no missed deliveries.
- The finance and accounting department tries to balance the objectives of minimum investment, low inventories, low capital equipment, and overhead.
- The engineering department attempts to reduce the product-development time.

The answer is striking the right balance in the short term as well as the long term. As a result, all of these potential conflicts must continually be addressed, evaluated, and changed if necessary. The key to making changes is the assurance that all levels in the organization have enough time to incorporate the changes in a timely, accurate, and cost-effective manner.

Your Assignment

Your first assignment as the Asset Manager's "Change Agent" is to review the competitive issues. As you look at each of these competitive issues, begin to list down in priority order which of these competitive issues you wish to gather details for a final presentation, which will be supported by a financial justification.

_____

_____

_____

_____

_____

_____

_____

_____

_____

_____

_____

_____

_____

ENVIRONMENTS AND THEIR EFFECTS ON ASSET MANAGEMENT

Business environments often determine the type of asset management systems needed in various industries. Following is a brief overview of the major types of business environments and their impact on financial and manufacturing systems.

The chart below illustrates that when product variety increases, the product volume decreases. The chart on the following page expands on this. Later chapters will deal with financial statement analysis of each of these major types of manufacturing environments.

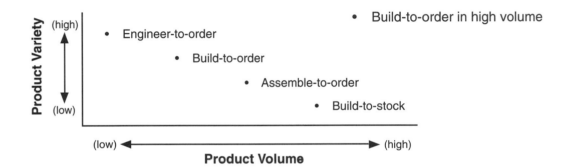

BUSINESS ENVIRONMENTS

Type of Business	Environment Description	Impact on Inventory
• Engineer-to-order	• Requires unique one-of-a-kind engineering design • Unique bill of materials and part # • Work does not begin until customer specifications are complete • Very long lead-time • One-of-a-kind products • High profit margin per unit	• No finished goods and little or no raw material until the customer specifications are complete
• Build-to-order	• More products than engineer-to-order; however, volumes are very low • Customer lead-times are long, but not as long as engineer-to-order • High profit margin per unit	• No finished goods • Raw material and work-in-process inventories • Safety stock carried for long lead-time items
• Assemble-to-order	• Fewer products produced than build-to-order, but volumes are higher • Build to forecasted options • Assemble option to customer specification • Use of planning bills • Medium profit margin per item	• Little if any finished goods • Inventory based on option forecast • Raw material held, especially for long lead-time items
• Build-to-stock	• Very low product variety, high product volume • Build to forecasted demand of independent items • Buffer for forecast error must be calculated • Low profit margins per item	• Inventory carried at the finished goods level • Emphasis on instant availability
• Build-to-order high volume	• Build-to-order high volume	• No inventory • Short lead-times

REVIEW QUESTIONS

The answers are on page 19.

1. List five reasons why assets should be managed.

    _____

    _____

    _____

    _____

    _____

2. List the most important competitive issues facing your company today.

    _____

    _____

    _____

3. What is the potential financial impact of not meeting the competitive issues discussion on the following items?

    *   Cash: _____

    *   Accounts Receivable: _____

    *   Inventory: _____

    *   Machinery and Equipment: _____

    *   Revenue/Sales: _____

    *   Expenses: _____

4. Consider the following examples of a cost reduction where the:

Unit Price is:	$20.00
Profit Margin is:	10%
Profit is:	2.00

If there were a direct material cost reduction of $2.00, the effect would be:

    I.   A reduction in the cost of goods sold of $200
    II. A doubling of the profit margin
    III. This $2.00 cost reduction would be equivalent to $20 in sales
    IV. The intangible cost would also increase

    A. All of the above
    B. I, II, and III
    C. II
    D. IV

5. Which of the following are major competitive issues facing businesses today?

    A. Improving forecast accuracy
    B. Better asset management
    C. Reducing cost
    D. Bringing products to market faster
    E. All of the above

6. In general, what is the impact on companies of producing products with increasingly shorter product life cycles?

    A. The break-even point will change if all other elements (revenues and cost) stay the same
    B. The "cash cow" dries up
    C. There is a probability any Engineering Change Orders (ECOs) will have a greater impact the later they are implemented
    D. All of the above

Answers: Review

1. Five reasons why assets should be managed. (Any of the following are considered correct.)

    1] Increase in profit; 2] Increase in Return on Assets [ROA]; 3] Increase in Return on Investments [ROI]; 4] Improve the cash position; 5] Reduce the costs; 6] Increase the revenue

2. List the most important competitive issues facing your company today. (Answers will vary by company.)

    1] Maximize customer service through improved forecasting; 2] Minimize inventory investment; 3] Maximize efficiency of purchasing and production; 4] Maximize profit; 5] Bring products to market faster; 6] Reduce costs; 7] Deliver high-quality products; 8] Improve employee training and education; 9] Develop informational organization; 10] Improve information exchange systems and networks

3. What is the potential financial impact of not meeting these competitive issues?

    Cash:

    1] Tied up in inventory; 2] Not available to pay debts

    Accounts Receivable:

    1] Poor quality can lead to longer time to collect; 2] Long time to collect impacts cash flowing into the company

    Inventory:

    1] Not having the correct type of inventory can lead to missed shipments, or even cancellation; 2] The larger the amount of inventory, the higher the potential for inventory becoming obsolete

    Machinery and Equipment:

    1] Using machinery and equipment before it is needed decreases its flexibility

    Revenue/Sales:

    1] Inaccurate sales/revenue forecast can lead to excess and obsolete inventory

    Expenses:

    1] Inaccurate revenue forecasts can lead to inventory write-offs, premiums and expedite charges 2] Poor quality can lead to rework and scrap charges

4. B

5. E

6. D

II

AN OVERVIEW OF FINANCIAL STATEMENTS AND THE ROLE OF ASSET MANAGEMENT

LEARNING OBJECTIVES

After completing this chapter, you will be able to:

- Define asset management

- Define the key components of the Balance Sheet and Income Statement

- Explain the ramifications of not managing assets

- Explain the key terms and definitions

- Define the difference between accounting and financial analysis

OVERVIEW OF FINANCIAL STATEMENTS
THE BALANCE SHEET

The first type of financial statement is the Balance Sheet. This statement shows assets, liabilities, and stockholders' equity.

Assets—Items the company owns. Assets are divided into short-term (consumed in less than a year) and long-term (has value for more than one year). Examples of short-term assets are cash, accounts receivable, and inventory. Examples of long-term assets are machines and equipment.

Liabilities—These are debts owed. Liabilities are divided into short-term and long-term. Short-term liabilities include accounts payable and taxes payable. Payments are due monthly. Long-term liabilities include the acquisition of buildings. Payments are spread out over more than one year.

Shareholders' Equity—Contains the value of the ownership of the stockholders (owners) and the earnings and losses the company has incurred since the company was started (retained earnings).

Asset Management Defined

For purposes of this book, asset management is defined as the comparison and reconciliation of the financial information of assets with the physical information of assets to ensure the highest possible return on these assets.

SAMPLE BALANCE SHEET

($Millions)

Current Assets	Current Year	Prior Year	Current Liabilities	Current Year	Prior Year
Cash	100	80	Accounts Payable	300	100
Accts. Receivable	200	160	Short-term debt	400	120
Inventories			Total Current Liabilities	700	220
Raw materials	100	60			
Work-in-process	400	60	Long-Term Liabilities		
Finished goods	215	90	Long-term debt	440	315
Total inventories	715	210	**TOTAL LIABILITIES**	**1,140**	**535**
Total Current Assets	**1,015**	**450**			
Property, Plant, and Equip.			**Stockholders' Equity**		
Land	50	45	Common stock	55	53
Buildings	340	220	Accumulated Retained		
Machinery, equip.,tools	610	535	Earnings	565	487
Total Property, Plant, and Equip.	**1,000**	**800**	**Total Stockholders' Equity**	**620**	**540**
Less accum. Depreciation	(255)	(175)			
Net Property, Plant, and Equip.	**745**	**625**	**TOTAL LIABILITIES AND STOCKHOLDERS' EQUITY**		
TOTAL ASSETS	**1,760**	**1,075**		**1,760**	**1,075**

Look at the Sample Balance Sheet above, at the amount of accounts receivables, inventories, and property, plant, and equipment—all non-cash assets. One quickly realizes why the management of these assets is so important. One also realizes why so many companies are moving/selling non-cash assets and working with contract manufacturing, and why contract manufacturing is one of the fastest growing industries in the world today.

Useful Tips for Reading a Balance Sheet

- The Balance Sheet is a statement—as of a specific date, for example, December 31—of what the company owns (assets), what it owes in debts (liabilities), and the difference between these two (assets minus liabilities), which is called the stockholders' equity (net worth).

- The assets are always listed in order of liquidity—how fast they could be turned into cash.

- The assets are divided into short-term assets (cash, short-term investments, accounts receivable, inventory, and so on) and long-term assets (machinery and equipment [less depreciation], facilities, land, and so on).

- The liabilities are always listed in the order in which the creditors would have claims against the assets should bankruptcy occur.

- Liabilities are broken into short-term liabilities—accounts payable, accrued payroll, short-term notes, and so on; and long-term liabilities—long-term debt, and so on.

- The total of the stockholders' equity section of the Balance Sheet must always represent the total assets minus total liabilities, so the following equation is always in balance:

Assets – Liabilities = Stockholders' Equity

This is commonly shown as the basic accounting equation:

Assets = Liabilities + Stockholders' Equity

- The stockholders' equity components are always listed in the order in which the stockholders would be paid after the creditors if the company were liquidated. For example, preferred stockholders would be paid before common stockholders.

- The retained earnings section of the stockholders' equity portion of the Balance Sheet represents the accumulation of all the profits and losses since the company's inception.

- Closing the books—when accountants talk about "closing the books" at month-end or year-end, they are referring to the accounting entry that "closes" the profit or loss for the year on the Income Statement and transferring this amount of profit or loss to the retained earnings portion of the Balance Sheet.

THE INCOME STATEMENT

The second type of financial statement is the Income Statement. This statement shows revenue (how much the company has earned year to date), Cost of Goods Sold (COGS) (how much it cost to produce the products sold), and Gross Profit (determined by subtracting the COGS from the revenue). All other expenses are included in the Sales, General, and Administrative Expenses (commonly referred to as SG&A). The net profit is determined by subtracting the SG&A expense from the Gross Profit.

Following is an example of an Income Statement.

SAMPLE INCOME STATEMENT

($Milllions)

	Current Year	Prior Year
Net Sales (Revenue)	**2,000**	**1,600**
Cost of Goods Sold and Operating Expenses		
Cost of goods sold	1,300	900
Gross profit	700	700
Sales, general, and administrative expenses (SG&A)	320	240
Operating Profit	380	460
Other Income (Expenses)		
Interest expense	(60)	(20)
Provision for Federal Income Taxes	(140)	(200)
Net Income	**180**	**240**

Useful Tips for Reading an Income Statement

- The Income Statement shows net sales less expenses, with the difference between the two (hopefully) being a profit (revenues greater than expenses).

- Net sales result from the sales of items that have been shipped from the Master Schedule.

- If discounts or allowances for quantity sales are granted, these amounts would be subtracted from the revenue line, and the result would be Net Sales.

- The expenses are divided into the major categories of Cost of Goods Sold (COGS), then Sales, General, and Administrative Expenses.

- The COGS includes the cost of the goods manufactured, which is made up of direct material, direct labor, and factory overhead.

- The difference between Net Sales and COGS is called the Gross Profit. The SG&A includes all other expenses not included in Cost of Goods Sold.

- The expenses for selling the product, general administrative expenses, and all other expenses are subtracted from the gross profit to give the profit before taxes or the loss the company incurred for the current one-year period.

- The profit (or loss) remaining after taxes is then transferred to retained earnings in the Balance Sheet when the books are closed for the year. The "books are closed."

ACCOUNTING VERSUS FINANCE— WHAT'S THE DIFFERENCE?

To begin with, accounting is the systematic recording of financial data according to the rules of Generally Accepted Accounting Principles (GAAP). Finance is the analysis of this information, with subsequent projections and recommendations. This book will emphasize the financial aspects of asset management.

Most of us envision assets as things such as bank accounts or gold mines. But what exactly is an asset? "An asset is anything that will contribute to a *positive cash flow* over time for a company."

Asset management, then, is the proper financial, as well as physical management of all of the company's assets, thus ensuring the maximum profit and return on assets/return on investment to ensure the highest possible earnings per share.

Viewed this way, any company has a wide array of extraordinary assets:

- Talented employees
- Technology (patents, know-how)
- Information
- Customer relationships
- Business reputation
- Cash
- Other non-cash "hard" assets (accounts receivable, inventory, machinery, and equipment)

The "non-financial" assets (the first five on the list) are very real and actually dwarf the last two, more commonly cited ones. The proof is simple. Consider the following example. The company had a net book value of approximately $430 million, but a market value of approximately $2 billion (almost five times). The inescapable conclusion is that the stock market, which is not an altruistic institution, perceives the company's value to be $1.6 billion in things the company owns *other than what shows up on its Balance Sheet.*

Nonetheless, the topic of how to create, nurture, and protect these valuable non-financial assets will be touched upon at the end of this book. In the meantime, however, there is still plenty for us to reflect on in the world of hard assets.

CATEGORIES OF HARD ASSETS

A glance at the Balance Sheet on page 24 reveals that most companies have lots of accounts receivable, inventory and so-called "fixed assets," such as machinery, equipment, and buildings. Very fortunately, some companies also have a large horde of "cash and securities." Companies can have so much cash for three reasons:

1. It has always been a wise policy to raise cash through equity issues (sales of stock) well in advance of any immediate need.

2. Most companies operate in very cyclical, competitive, and technologically turbulent industries. It pays to carry excess cash against a "rainy day."

3. Companies are increasingly interested in acquiring complementary companies and technologies. Having the cash on hand is a competitive advantage against other potential suitors.

As fascinating as cash management is, it is not the main topic of this book. Some companies maintain a small but highly skilled treasury department that, working with outside money managers, makes the necessary trade-offs of yield, asset risk, and instrument duration. Many times interest income contributes as much as 15 cents per share per year to earnings.

Accounts Receivable

Accounts Receivable (A/R) is best measured by looking *backward* from a Balance Sheet date to see how many recent periods' revenue is still uncollected. DSOs are a quick, *approximate* measure of how quickly a company collects on credit shipments.

The most common measure is "Days' Sales Outstanding" or DSOs:

$$\text{DSO} = \frac{\text{A/R on B/S} \quad \times \quad 91 \text{ (days in a quarter; 365 days for annualized calculation)}}{\text{Net Sales (for the period under review)}}$$

DSOs are a reflection of many aspects of a company's performance:

- How satisfied customers are

- How smoothly the sales and collection administrations function

- Whether the company chooses to recognize revenue early or late in the range considered acceptable under Generally Accepted Accounting Principles (GAAP)

- How linear shipments are over the quarter

- Quality

DSOs vary widely across industries and even across companies within a given industry. The fast-food industry is an example. McDonald's has very low DSOs (no one buys a hamburger except with cash). Most industries have DSOs somewhere between 30 and 70 days. The semiconductor capital equipment industry tends to be outside this range. Typically these companies have DSOs of about 90 days. From the cash-collection side of A/R, most companies make their life even more difficult by:

- Selling "bleeding-edge" technology that has not been thoroughly debugged by engineering and manufacturing.

- Having information flow unevenly from the field installation teams to engineering, manufacturing, sales, or collections.

- Recognizing revenue when the customer agrees, *in the factory*, that the system works (as opposed to waiting for them to agree some time later that the system works *in their factory*).

- Shipments vary toward quarter-end.

These are the issues to be alert to whenever DSOs rise.

Inventory

Inventory is best measured by looking *forward* from a Balance Sheet date to see how many future periods' shipments can be built with the inventory currently on hand. The standard measure is "turns":

$$\text{Turns} = \frac{\text{Next Quarter's COGS} \times 4}{\text{Current Inventory}} \quad \text{or} \quad \frac{\text{Annual COGS}}{\text{Current Inventory}}$$

In other words, if the company shipped for the next year at the rate next quarter is expected to achieve, how many times would inventory have to be replenished? The higher the turns, the better. High turns means that, for a given sale level, the company can operate with a low investment in inventory.

Below is a list of potential items that might impact the inventory turns.

- Marketing's ability to forecast orders and, therefore, revenues

- Based on the marketing forecast, determine (and control) the timing of parts deliveries

- Manufacturing's ability to stay on schedule

- How well the materials planning software systems, as well as the financial system, reconcile

- How aggressively management reviews and dispositions "excess and obsolete" inventory

- The length of the "lead/cycle time" to build product

- How many options the company chooses to offer customers

- How much "safety stock" the company chooses to keep

- How many "non-manufacturing" systems management chooses to keep on hand (for example, for engineering development, customer demos or loaners, field service training, and so on)

Evaluating Turns

Inventory turns also vary across and within industries. For example, retailers typically have turns in the range of ten to fourteen. Capital equipment manufacturers' turns are much lower—in the range of two to three. The PC industry has one of the highest turns since it builds not to forecast but only against actual orders. Turns vary dramatically across product lines depending on all the factors listed above.

In general, when turns fall, management needs to ask itself:

- Are we allowing so many customer changes that inventory is becoming obsolete before its even shipped?

- Is this a temporary blip due to revenue "lumpiness"?

- Are we taking a realistic view of bookings and revenue, or do we just believe our own "wishful thinking"?

- Is the complex manufacturing system bogging down (cycle time, MRP, customer changes)?

- Are we adequately attacking (and reserving for) excess and obsolete parts?

- Do we fully understand the costs of complexity (options) and immediate demand fulfillment (safety stock)?

When turns drop, Wall Street analysts (correctly) become very leery of reported results because experience has taught them that some of that inventory "assets" will shortly be written off as an "adjustment." Unfortunately, most companies have had ample opportunity to make the same discovery.

Fixed Assets: Machinery and Equipment

Fixed assets are multi-year assets, unlike A/R or inventory, which are supposed to (but don't always) turn over in a matter of months. There is no single ratio that works for everyone. Perhaps the most common measure is to compare capital spending over one year to sales. Examples of capital-intensive industries are oil refining, automobiles, and semiconductor manufacturers.

Since fixed assets are multi-year in nature, they are potentially subject to both operating and accounting abuse. In other words, the "buyer" does not always adequately appreciate the burden of future depreciation charges and the accountant sometimes exaggerates its useful life. On the other hand, fixed assets can sometimes be much more efficient than leases or rentals where one can fall into the trap of "buying" the same asset several times over its active life.

Many companies' main capital needs are computers (to run the factory and also for each desktop) and buildings (the basic structures, clean-rooms, and myriad other "improvements").

Contract manufacturing is one of the major contributing factors to a company's decrease in machinery and equipment (M&E) investments. The strategy to "outsource" to contract manufacturers frees up cash investments in people, inventory, machinery, equipment, and buildings, which frees up tremendous amounts of assets to invest in research and development to bring new products to market even faster.

WHEN RATIOS CHANGE: FINDING THE CAUSE

When the ratio of capital spending to sales rises, management needs to determine which of the following is the real root cause:

- Our business has actually become more capital-intensive

- By its very nature, capital spending is lumpy and we are just catching up

- We have unduly lowered the threshold for capital spending and we are not treating it as the P&L expense it ultimately will turn out to be (because of depreciation)

- We haven't fully implemented the contract manufacturing strategy

Keep a Watchful Eye on Assets

Smart investors watch balance sheets very carefully. Employees (who are "investing" their time and their career prospects in a company) should likewise keep a sharp eye on the Balance Sheet and should demand top-notch asset performance from themselves and from all levels of management. Remember: The Balance Sheet is only a way-station for non-cash assets, all of which end up in one of two final resting places:

- Good, collectible A/R, which becomes *cash*.

- *All* other assets end up as *expenses*.

There is no third exit from this turnpike!

Cash-to-Cash

The concept of cash-to-cash deals initially with the speed at which inventory can be turned into accounts receiveable, and subsequently into cash. The second concept is the time it takes to pay the accounts payable.

In a manufacturing company, one of the major factors that influence cash-to-cash is the inventory investment. This investment is reflected in the days' supply of inventory at any time during the course of the year. This cash-to-cash concept is expanded upon later.

Vendor Managed Inventory

Vendor Managed Inventory (VMI) is a concept which, through negotiations, the supplier agrees to hold inventory until needed by the customer. VMI agreements vary from situation to situation. At one end of the spectrum, the supplier holds the inventory in its facilities at no cost to the customer, and is paid when the customer uses the inventory. At the other end, the supplier simply provides the inventory at a customer-designated location at no cost to the customer and the customer is billed when the inventory is used.

ALLOCATION OF FACTORY OVERHEAD AND ACTIVITY-BASED COSTING

In many companies, the total factory overhead is growing faster than the other major COGS items—for example, direct labor and direct material. In the past, these overhead costs had been allocated to products or product lines based on direct labor or machine run-time per units, subassembly, assembly, and so on. But because of significant reduction in direct labor content and changes in machine technology, a new method of allocating overhead was required. This method was called *activity-based costing*. When coupled with the concept of cost drivers, a more equitable way of allocating overhead costs resulted. Examples of cost drivers are head count, complexity of the preparation of the purchase order (PO), line items on a PO, and so on.

The result of using activity-based costing does not change the overall profit or loss of a company, but it does more fairly allocate a major component of COGS—overhead—thus presenting a more precise statement of product-line profitability.

Inventory Valuation

The actual value of inventory using generally accepted accounting principles is computed using one of three basic approaches: first-in-first-out (FIFO), last-in-first-out (LIFO), or a standard cost. In project or government orders, actual costs are charged directly to work being performed (work orders). This method is sometimes called "order-specific costing" and is usually used when large, expensive items or projects are involved.

Some companies inadvertently use an inventory system called "FISH"—first-in-still-here. The author does not recommend this!

Note that the above accounting methods are used only to value the inventory on the Balance Sheet and the Income Statement, not to determine the sequence in which material is used.

FIFO assumes inventory leaves in the same order as it arrives; oldest goods leave first. LIFO assumes the most recent arrivals in inventory are consumed first. In other words, the last items into inventory are the first to be charged to the COGS.

In FIFO, inventory on the Balance Sheet is based on the newest parts to come in; in LIFO it is the oldest item.

Valuing inventory at standard cost involves recording the inventory on the Balance Sheet and COGS at a predetermined rate for material, direct labor, and overhead. These predetermined rates are called *standards*. If significant variances occur between actual prices, the inventory and COGS are adjusted up or down. The accounting department usually does this on a monthly or quarterly basis.

Inventory is valued at either its original cost or its current market value, whichever is lower. This conservative accounting approach gives recognition to the fact that inventory values can change with time and can decrease in value because of such factors as time, obsolescence, and so on.

EXERCISE 1

In the following exercise, determine the value of the inventory, using LIFO, FIFO, and standard cost. The answers are on page 46.

PURCHASES

Months	Quantity	Unit Cost
January	1000	$4.00
February	2000	4.20
March	1000	4.20
April	1500	4.40
May	1000	4.50
June	2000	4.50
Total	**8500**	

Beginning on-hand inventory = 0

4000 units were being sold during the first half of the year.

Standard cost: $4.40

Determine the value of the 4000 units using LIFO, FIFO, and standard cost.

_____

_____

_____

_____

_____

_____

_____

_____

_____

_____

_____

_____

_____

DETERMINING OTHER COSTS

There are additional costs associated with inventory, which include the cost to order, carry and store, stock-out, and transport inventory; as well as the costs of the inventory not being available when needed. Following is a summary of these costs and examples of each.

Ordering/Set-Up Costs

- Clerical work of preparing, issuing, following, and receiving orders
- Physical handling of goods
- Inspection
- Machine set-ups (if manufactured)

Carrying Costs

- Obsolescence
- Deterioration
- Taxes (in some localities)
- Insurance
- Storage
- Capital

The cost of carrying inventory is usually defined as a percentage of dollar value of inventory per unit of time (generally one year).

Storage Costs

- Utilities
- Warehouse/stock-room personnel
- Maintenance of building and equipment
- Warehouse security
- Returned Material Authorization (RMAs)
- Engineering Change Orders (ECOs)

Stock-out Costs

- Expediting costs

- Freight premiums

- Back-order processing

- Difficult to determine because of intangible costs such as lost sales and customer goodwill

Transportation Costs

- Inventory tied up in transit

- Spoilage

- Damage

- Insurance

- Theft

- Handling

EXERCISE 2

From the following information construct a Balance Sheet and an Income Statement. The answers are on page 47.

($Millions)

Accounts Receivable	148
Cash & Securities	242
Cost of Goods Sold	455
Current Liabilities	130
Fixed Assets	54
Inventory	93
Long-Term Liabilities	9
Net Sales	600
Sales, General, & Administrative	30
Stockholders' Equity	398

In the space below, prepare a:

Balance Sheet

Income Statement

KEY FINANCIAL RATIOS

The following charts show the major calculations of key financial ratios: liquidity, leverage, and profitability. Within each of these categories are examples of the ratios, methods of calculations, and a short list of industry standards and their significance.

A ratio shows one number's (current assets) relationship to another (current liabilities). For example, if the current ratio were two-to-one, this would reflect the fact that for every $1 worth of liabilities, there would be $2 worth of assets. Look for the key terms in the Balance Sheet (BS) and Income Statement (IS).

KEY FINANCIAL RATIOS

Name	Method of Calculation	Standard & Significance	
LIQUIDITY			
Current Ratio	$\dfrac{\text{Current Assets (BS)}}{\text{Current Liabilities (BS)}}$	Industry average: Low—possible cash flow problems. High—might not be managing assets, such as inventory well.	↑
Quick Ratio	$\dfrac{\text{Cash Through Receivables (BS)}}{\text{Current Liabilities (BS)}}$	Low—cash flow problems. High—might mean poor asset management.	↑
Days' Sales Outstanding (DSO)	$\dfrac{\text{Receivables} \times 365 \text{ (BS)}}{\text{Net Sales (IS)}}$	High hurts cash flow. Very low—too restrictive credit policies.	↓
Inventory Turnover (Turns)	$\dfrac{\text{Cost of Goods Sold (IS)}}{\text{Inventory (BS)}}$	Industry average: Low—problems with slow inventory that might hurt cash flow. Very high—might run out of inventory.	↑
Days' Supply Of Inventory	$\dfrac{365 \text{ Days}}{\text{Inventory Turns}}$	The lower the better. Remember, the maximum amount of inventory that can be shipped is one day's worth.	↓
Days' Payables Outstanding	$\dfrac{\text{Payables} \times 365 \text{ (BS)}}{\text{Cost of Goods Sold (IS)}}$	Industry average: Indicates how long the company takes to pay its bills.	↕
LEVERAGE			
Debt-to-Equity	$\dfrac{\text{Total Liabilities (BS)}}{\text{Stockholders' Equity (BS)}}$	Industry average: Debt the company has incurred compared to Stockholders' Equity.	↕
PROFITABILITY			
Return on Equity	$\dfrac{\text{Net Income (IS)}}{\text{Stockholders' Equity (BS)}}$	The higher the better. The return on the shareholders' investment in the business.	↑
Return on Assets	$\dfrac{\text{Net Income (IS)}}{\text{Total Assets (BS)}}$	Industry average: Return the company earns on everything it owns.	↑

EXERCISE 3

Using the company's financial statements on pages 40 and 41, calculate the following ratios (round all decimals back two places). The answers are on page 48.

KEY FINANCIAL RATIOS

Name	Method of Calculation	Current Year	Prior Year
Liquidity Current Ratio	$\dfrac{\text{Current Assets}}{\text{Current Liabilities}}$		
Quick Ratio	$\dfrac{\text{Cash Through Receivables}}{\text{Current Liabilities}}$		
Days Sales Outstanding	$\dfrac{\text{Receivables x 365}}{\text{Net Sales}}$		
Inventory Turnover (Turns)	$\dfrac{\text{Cost of Goods Sold}}{\text{Inventory}}$		
Days' Supply of Inventory	$\dfrac{\text{365 Days}}{\text{Inventory Turns}}$		
Days' Payables Outstanding	$\dfrac{\text{Payables x 365}}{\text{Cost of Goods Sold}}$		
Leverage Debt-to-Equity	$\dfrac{\text{Total Liabilities}}{\text{Equity}}$		
Profitability Return on Equity	$\dfrac{\text{Net Income}}{\text{Equity}}$		
Return on Assets	$\dfrac{\text{Net Income}}{\text{Total Assets}}$		

SAMPLE BALANCE SHEET

($Millions)

	Current Year	Prior Year		Current Year	Prior Year
Current Assets			**Current Liabilities**		
Cash	1,100	900	Accounts Payable	505	400
Accts. Receivable	1,445	1,200	Short-term debt	200	300
Inventories			Total Current Liabilities	705	700
Raw materials	0	110			
Work-in-process	10	40	Long-Term Liabilities		
Finished goods	230	310	Long-term debt	60	79
Total inventories	240	460	**TOTAL LIABILITIES**	**765**	**779**
Total Current Assets	**2,785**	**2,560**			
Property, Plant, and Equip.			**Stockholders' Equity**		
Land	160	100	Common stock	665	588
Buildings	340	220	Accumulated Retained		
Machinery, equip.,tools	400	900	Earnings	2,000	1,663
Total Property, Plant, and Equip.	**900**	**1,220**	**Total Stockholders' Equity**	**2,665**	**2,251**
Less accum. Depreciation	(255)	(750)			
Net Property, Plant, and Equip.	**645**	**470**	**TOTAL LIABILITIES AND STOCKHOLDERS' EQUITY**		
TOTAL ASSETS	**3,430**	**3,030**		**3,430**	**3,030**

SAMPLE INCOME STATEMENT

($Milllions)

	Current Year	Prior Year
Net Sales (Revenue)	**8,500**	**7,100**
Cost of Goods Sold and Operating Expenses		
Cost of goods sold	4,300	3,900
Gross profit	4,200	3,200
Sales, general, and administrative expenses (SG&A)	2,400	1,800
Operating Profit	1,800	1,400
Other Income (Expenses)		
Interest expense	(60)	(60)
Net Income Before Taxes	1740	1340
Provision for Federal Income Taxes	(740)	(540)
Net Income	1,000	800

THE BASIC ACCOUNTING/MANUFACTURING FORMULA

The basic accounting formulas (dollars) and the basic manufacturing formula (units) must be tied together. Dollars and units must support the company's long-term, medium-term, and short-term revenue and production objectives.

During the business planning process, sales are forecasted. This long-to-medium-term sales forecast is based on desired market share, competitive issues, economic conditions, and sales projections. The sales forecasts also include forecasts for service parts and special promotions. Internal requirements for distribution, interplant orders, engineering orders, inventory build-ups, and safety stocks should also be considered. The end result is the total production to meet project revenue and inventory levels for the coming year.

The formula below will help you visualize how business planning drives the financial planning, as well as manufacturing planning of the company.

THE BASIC ACCOUNTING/MANUFACTURING FORMULA

Step		Basic Accounting Manufacturing Formula	Units	Dollars (Millions)
4		Beginning inventory	1,000	$1,000
5	+	Production levels (build plan)	9,500	9,500
3	=	Available inventory to ship (at cost)	10,500	10,500
1	–	Shipments/Sales (cost of goods sold)	10,000	10,000
2	=	Ending inventory	500	500

FORECASTING REVENUE

The forecasted revenue is the first step in making sure basic manufacturing and accounting formulas discussed earlier are in balance and there are adequate financial resources to support the projected inventory and shipment levels. Following are the steps in this process:

STEP 1 First there is a need to establish projected shipments/sales for the year. Top executives establish the sales levels required to meet the business objectives relative to growth, market share, and so on. In this example, the projected shipment is 10,000 units with a cost of $1,000,000. This figure would be increased by the gross profit percentage to arrive at the forecasted revenue and increase or decrease to accounts receivable.

STEP 2 Next, the ending inventory levels must be set. Inventory levels are based on two requirements:

- The desired level of customer satisfaction (that is, how many times you can ship when the customer wants the product shipped).
- Forecast error, which refers to the difference between forecasted sales and actual sales.

In this example, the projected (forecasted) ending inventory level is 500 units.

STEP 3 When you have determined the desired level of shipments and have projected the ending inventory levels, you can determine the available inventory units to ship by adding the shipment of 10,000 units to the projected (forecasted) ending inventory level of 500 units.

STEP 4 The beginning inventory for the year is taken directly from the ending inventory of the previous year. In this example, it is 1,000 units.

STEP 5 You can now determine the production for the year by subtracting the beginning inventory (1,000 units) from the available-to-ship inventory (10,500 units). In this example, the production is 9,500 units.

STEP 6 Finally, the production plan must be compared to the financial resources committed to fund this production. Major expenditures such as buildings, machinery, and equipment, head-count increases, and material acquisition plans must be budgeted. The determination of whether or not the company can fund this level of revenue is reviewed. If there is sufficient cash the plan is approved. If there is not sufficient cash, alternative plans need to be made.

REVIEW QUESTIONS

See page 49 for the answers.

1. Asset Management is defined as:

    A. Items the company owns

    B. The value of the net worth

    C. A and B

    D. Proper financial and physical management of the company's assets

2. The Balance Sheet is:

    A. How much the company earned year-to-date

    B. Debts owed

    C. Items company owns

    D. Statement of assets, liabilities, and stockholders' equity

3. Gross Profit is the:

    A. Bottom line profit or loss

    B. Revenue greater than COGS

    C. Profit less SG&A

    D. None of the above

4. Assets:

    A. Must equal liabilities plus stockholders' equity

    B. Are things the company owns

    C. Are divided between short-term and long-term

    D. All of the above

5. When the books are "closed":

    A. The company is bankrupt

    B. Net profit or loss on the income statement is transferred to the retained earnings in the stockholders' equity

    C. Neither A or B

    D. Both A and B

6. Redo this P&L statement, given a 4% reduction in COGS. Calculate the percentage of profit improve ment? (Profit Margin: 40% (400,000 / 1,000,000; Tax rate: 30%; Assume: 4% COGS Reduction)

	A	B
Annual sales	1,000,000	1,000,000
COGS	- 600,000	
Gross profit	400,000	
SG&A	- 250,000	- 250,000
Earnings before taxes	150,000	
Taxes	- 45,000	
Earnings after taxes	105,000	

Answers: Exercise 1

PURCHASES

LIFO		Cost of Goods Sold	Inventory Value
June	2000 x 4.50 =	$9,000	
May	1000 x 4.50 =	4,500	
April	1000 x 4.40 =	4,400	
April	500 x 4.40 =		$2,200
March	1000 x 4.20 =		4,200
February	2000 x 4.20 =		8,400
January	1000 x 4.00 =		4,000
		$17,900	**$18,800**

FIFO		Cost of Goods Sold	Inventory Value
January	1000 x 4.00 =	$4,000	
February	2000 x 4.20 =	8,400	
March	1000 x 4.20 =	4,200	
April	1500 x 4.40 =		6,600
May	1000 x 4.50 =		4,500
June	2000 x 4.50 =		9,000
		$16,600	**$20,100**

Standard Cost:

Total purchases 8,500 units

$4.40 x 4000 = $17,600 - Cost of Goods Sold

$4.40 x 4500 = $19,800 - Inventory Value

Answers: Exercise 2

BALANCE SHEET

($Millions)

Cash & Securities	242
Accounts Receivable	148
Inventory	93
Fixed Assets	54
Total Assets	**537**
Current Liabilities	130
Long-Term Liabilities	9
Total Liabilities	**139**
Stockholders' Equity	**398**
Total Liabilities & Stockholders' Equity	**537**

INCOME STATEMENT

Net Sales	600
Cost of Goods Sold	-455
Gross Profit	145
SG&A	30
Profit	**115**

Answers: Exercise 3

Does your completed table look like this?

KEY FINANCIAL RATIOS
(Round all decimals back two places)

Name	Method of Calculation	Current Year	Prior Year
Liquidity Current Ratio	$\dfrac{\text{Current Assets}}{\text{Current Liabilities}}$	$\dfrac{2785}{705}$ = 3.95	$\dfrac{2560}{700}$ = 3.66
Quick Ratio	$\dfrac{\text{Cash Through Receivables}}{\text{Current Liabilities}}$	$\dfrac{1100 + 1445}{705}$ = 3.61	$\dfrac{900 + 1200}{700}$ = 3.00
Days Sales Outstanding	$\dfrac{\text{Receivables x 365}}{\text{Net Sales}}$	$\dfrac{1445 \times 365}{8500}$ = 62.05	$\dfrac{1200 \times 365}{7100}$ = 61.69
Inventory Turnover	$\dfrac{\text{Cost of Goods Sold}}{\text{Inventory}}$	$\dfrac{4300}{240}$ = 17.90	$\dfrac{3900}{460}$ = 8.48
Days' Supply of Inventory	$\dfrac{\text{365 Days}}{\text{Inventory Turns}}$	$\dfrac{365}{17.9}$ = 20.39	$\dfrac{365}{8.48}$ = 43.04
Days' Payable Outstanding	$\dfrac{\text{Payables x 365}}{\text{Cost of Goods Sold}}$	$\dfrac{505 \times 365}{4300}$ = 42.87	$\dfrac{400 \times 365}{3900}$ = 37.44
Leverage Debt-to-Equity	$\dfrac{\text{Total Liabilities}}{\text{Stockholders' Equity}}$	$\dfrac{765}{2665}$ = 0.29	$\dfrac{779}{2251}$ = 0.35
Profitability Return on Equity	$\dfrac{\text{Net Income Before Taxes}}{\text{Stockholders' Equity}}$	$\dfrac{1740}{2665}$ = 0.65	$\dfrac{1340}{2251}$ = 0.60
Return on Assets	$\dfrac{\text{Net Income Before Taxes}}{\text{Total Assets}}$	$\dfrac{1740}{3430}$ = 0.51	$\dfrac{1340}{3030}$ = 0.44

Answers: Review

1. D

2. D

3. B

4. D

5. B

6. The numbers in your P&L should read as follows:

	A	B
Annual sales	1,000,000	1,000,000
COGS	- 600,000	- 576,000
Gross profit	400,000	424,000
SG&A	- 250,000	- 250,000
Earnings before taxes	150,000	174,000
Taxes	- 45,000	- 52,200
Earnings after taxes	105,000	121,800

Result: A 16% profit improvement.

CHAPTER

III

TYING FINANCIAL INFORMATION TO MANUFACTURING INFORMATION

LEARNING OBJECTIVES

After completing this chapter, you will be able to:

- List the major components of the key financial statements
- Explain the key terms and definitions
- Complete a financial analysis

PART 1—FORECASTING, MASTER SCHEDULING, AND CAPACITY MANAGEMENT TO NET SALES AND A/R

MANUFACTURING RESOURCE PLANNING

Below is the closed-loop MRPII/ERP system. This figure represents the major modules that most software providers of manufacturing systems encompass. This also shows the major related financial modules such as sales, Accounts Receivable, cost of goods sold (COGS), inventory, and so on. These items are highlighted below and will be the starting point for the discussions to follow.

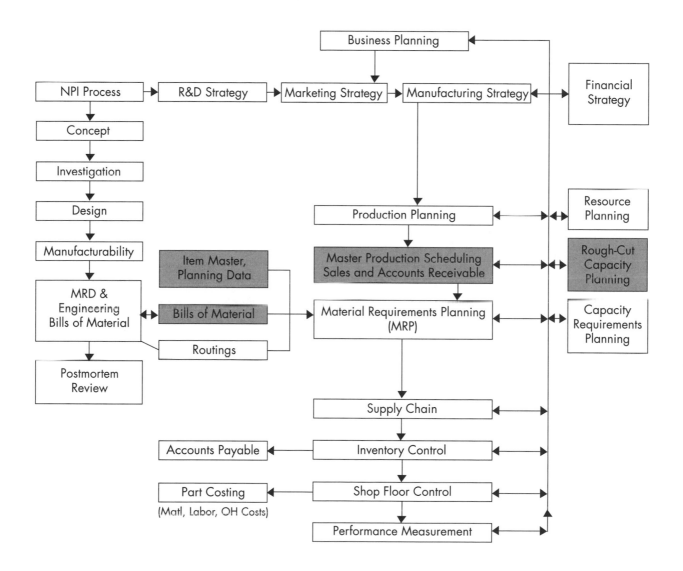

TYING FINANCIAL INFORMATION TO MANUFACTURING INFORMATION

From the MRPII/ERP systems shown on the prior page, the following key items are shown on the chart below. This chart shows the relationship of the financial systems with the manufacturing systems.

Cash Flow	Financial System	Manufacturing System	Inventory Flow
Cash Comes In	Net Sales & Accounts Receivable	= Master Schedule	Inventory Goes Out
	Cost of Goods Sold & Inventory	= Material Requirements Planning	
	Costed Bill of Material	= Bill of Material	
Cash is Tied Up	Inventory (Raw Material, Work-in-Process)	= Inventory Management & Shop Floor Control	Inventory is Tied Up
Cash Goes Out	Accounts Payable	= Inventory Purchases	Inventory Comes In

Now let's look at each of these in more detail. This chapter will examine net sales, Accounts Receivable, as well as the Master Schedule and forecasts.

Net Sales and Accounts Receivable

When the product ships and net sales are recognized, the job of collecting Accounts Receivable begins. The Accounts Receivable is ordinarily turned into cash based on the terms of payment. A common basis for terms of payment is 2/10, net 30, which says if the payment is made in 10 days or less, the customer is entitled to a 2% discount, otherwise the invoice payment is due in 30 days from the shipment or customer acceptance.

There are reasons, however, when payment is not made within the prescribed period of time. Following is a list of reasons payments might not be made within the payment term, thus having a negative impact on cash flow.

- The customer's business, or the economy in general, might be slow and they look for reasons not to pay.
- There could be recently discovered quality problems.
- There could be disputes over the interpretation of terms and conditions.
- The letter of credit might have expired.

All of the above items not only impact cash flowing into the company, but they also prolong the time cash is tied up to pay for things such as inventory.

Inventory and Accounts Payable

Cash flows out of the company in many different ways. However, if you were to look at most manufacturing companies' Balance Sheets, you would see inventory as one of the biggest cash outlays.

The acquisition of inventory increases the inventory on the asset side of the Balance Sheet and increases the Accounts Payable on the liability side of the Balance Sheet.

The actual cash outlay doesn't take place until the goods are received, inspected, and then authorized for payment. Some companies make it a practice to prolong payments as long as possible, thus postponing the cash outlay (negative cash flow). If all goes well, payments to the supplier are made within the company's stated payment terms, which is typically 2/10, net 30.

Once the payment is made to the supplier, every attempt should be made to build the inventory, as soon as possible, and ship it to the customer.

Capacity Planning

Before making commitments to the customer or to the forecast, the Master Schedule is checked against available capacity.

This checking process, also known as *rough-cut capacity planning*, first calculates critical resources, such as bottleneck machinery, labor shortages, and material shortages. This process produces a report called the rough-cut capacity plan, which shows any shortfalls of capacity of critical resources. This entire process has cash implications, in so far as Purchasing places orders with suppliers, and Production schedules, material, people, and machinery. Accounting prepares cash flow analysis and other financial reports.

If there are no imbalances between the load of the projected sales/revenue and the available capacity, then the plan is ready for execution.

Once the Master Schedule has been checked and there is enough capacity, the Material Requirements Plan (MRP) explosion takes place.

The MRP determines a time-phased schedule of materials required to produce the units to be sold to make the revenue plan. The financial ramifications of the MRP will be discussed in the next chapter.

FINANCIAL IMPACT OF INSUFFICIENT CAPACITY

Failure to ensure that the checks and balances between Master Scheduling and rough-cut capacity planning can result in missed shipments, low customer satisfaction, and higher inventories. Sales, accounts receivable, and cash collections will happen on a timely basis only if there is enough capacity.

If there are more orders than capacity available to build, inventory and lead-times will increase and inventory turns and potentially ROA will decrease.

Failure to balance out the high-level production and resource plans will cause problems throughout the rest of the planning and execution process. The objectives of medium-term plans contained in the Master Schedule and the short-term plans contained in the MRP will not be achieved.

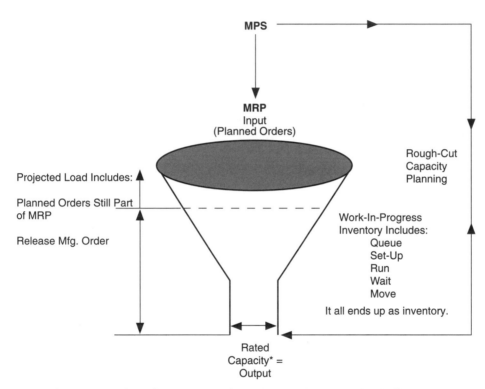

MPS

MRP
Input
(Planned Orders)

Rough-Cut
Capacity
Planning

Projected Load Includes:

Planned Orders Still Part
of MRP

Release Mfg. Order

Work-In-Progress
Inventory Includes:
Queue
Set-Up
Run
Wait
Move

It all ends up as inventory.

Rated
Capacity* =
Output

* Capacity equals Output (order completions): Anything more than one days' worth of inventory equals
  potential excess of inventory.

The process produces a report called the *rough-cut capacity plan*, which shows any shortfalls of capacity of critical resources.

If there are no imbalances between the load of the projected sales/revenue and the available capacity, the plan is ready for execution.

THE MASTER SCHEDULE

From the manufacturing side of the formula, master scheduling and demand management involve:

- receiving customer orders
- determining forecasted shipment levels
- setting the finished goods inventory level
- developing a Master Schedule
- testing the Master Schedule through rough-cut capacity planning

Remember the Master Schedule shows ship dates—not order-entry dates. These ship dates are based on lead-times, which are based on "complete" orders. One of the major contributing factors to missed shipments is because ship dates are given but the customer orders are still incomplete. This has tremendous financial costs.

From the financial side of the formula, Master Scheduling and Demand Management determine the revenue and the accounts receivable when the shipments take place. In addition, this information may also be included in the cost input side of the cash-flow analysis.

The forecasting portion of the Master Schedule can provide stability to material planning by increasing the forecast accuracy and reducing the schedule "nervousness." As a result, costly expediting, as well as inventory investments, can be minimized. This not only impacts cash flows, but improves inventory turns as well.

In addition to forecasts and customer orders, this schedule contains the *available-to-promise* and *projected available inventory balances*. The output of the Master Schedule is the line called the Master Production Schedule (MPS). The amounts of this line are used to drive the Material Requirements Plan (MRP). (The following pages will focus on the forecasted sales and customer orders.)

TYPICAL MASTER SCHEDULE

The figure below is an example of a Master Schedule.

<table>
<tr><td colspan="7">Jade Ink
Master Schedule</td></tr>
<tr><td colspan="7">Item: 1645ASTER</td></tr>
<tr><td colspan="4">Description: Pen</td><td colspan="3">* Demand Fence 4</td></tr>
<tr><td colspan="4">Planning Horizon: 6 periods</td><td colspan="3">Lot Size – 1000</td></tr>
<tr><td>Period</td><td>1</td><td>2</td><td>3</td><td>4</td><td>5</td><td>6</td></tr>
<tr><td>Forecasted Sales</td><td></td><td></td><td></td><td>340</td><td>240</td><td>280</td></tr>
<tr><td>Customer Orders</td><td>380</td><td>400</td><td>300</td><td></td><td></td><td></td></tr>
<tr><td>*Projected Available Balance (PAB)
(Beginning Inventory)   800</td><td>420</td><td>20</td><td>720</td><td>380</td><td>1140</td><td>860</td></tr>
<tr><td>*Available-to-Promise</td><td>20</td><td></td><td>700</td><td></td><td>1000</td><td></td></tr>
<tr><td>Master Production Schedule</td><td></td><td></td><td>1000</td><td></td><td>1000</td><td></td></tr>
<tr><td></td><td></td><td></td><td>▼</td><td></td><td>▼</td><td></td></tr>
</table>

Explosion into MRP

The final two lines are the projected available balance (PAB) and the available-to-promise (ATP) line.

Available-to-promise represents the unsold capacity, the capacity to produce units to be sold to customers. This calculation can be period by period or it can be stated as a cumulative amount.

ATP is the uncommitted inventory balance in the first period and is normally calculated for each period in which an MPS receipt is scheduled. In the first period ATP includes on-hand inventory less customer orders. The formula[†] = for ATP is:

Beginning Inventory (in first period only) + MPS – the sum

of the customer orders before the next MPS.

The formula for the Projected Available Balance is:

Before the Demand Time Fence:

Prior period PAB + MPS – customer orders = PAB

After the Demand Time Fence:

Prior period PAB + MPS – Forecast or customer order (whichever is greater) = PAB.

---

[*] PAB represents the inventory balance projected into the future. This will be covered in the next chapter.

[†] A more detailed description of these formulas can be found in *Just in Time Forecasting and Master Scheduling*, by Dave Viale.

DEVELOPING A FORECASTING MODEL

The forecasted sales included in the Master Schedule are usually stated as a monthly rate. For planning purposes, the rate must be expressed in units identical to those in the production plan described in prior pages. Master Schedules must also include the dollar amounts of the individual forecasted product sales.

The sales forecast represents sales and marketing management's best estimate of future orders. Customer orders and forecasts of future customer orders (when combined with service parts, interplant orders, and warehouse needs) equal the shipment levels for the coming months, quarters, or years. This demand is referred to as independent demand (coming from *outside* the production factory). The Master Schedule's accuracy or inaccuracy can have very large financial implications.

Improved forecasting models reduce the amount of forecast error and create fewer stock-outs. Reducing the forecast error enables you to reduce inventory, as well as freeing up additional resources, such as cash.

Simple forecasting models frequently provide results that are nearly as good as the more complex ones. The more elaborate mathematical models are useful only if non-technical users can understand them and make appropriate decisions based on the results.

Forecasting Objectives

Forecasting answers the question of when orders will come in, how much inventory is needed to buffer fluctuations in forecast, customer demand, customer change orders, and supplier deliveries. If done correctly, forecasting will support the other production and supply-chain management objectives. The forecasting tools and concepts presented here support contract manufacturing as well.

The major reason for any type of forecasting is to reconcile these potentially conflicting objectives mentioned earlier:

- maximize customer service
- maximize efficiency of purchasing, production, and indirect labor
- minimize inventory investment
- maximize profit

Reconciling these factors will bring increasing return on investment (ROI) and return on assets (ROA).

PAYING FOR CHANGES

Whoever causes the changes pays for the changes! Anyway you look at it, it's going to impact someone's "bottom line" or "top line."

It is very important to determine what caused the change and the related costs (premiums, expediting, transportation, and so on).

- If customers cause the change they should pay.
- If suppliers cause the change they should pay.
- If the company caused the change it should pay.

Not recouping this cost of change from customers and suppliers is one of the major contributors to the "hidden cost of manufacturing" and the subsequent erosion of profit margins. In situations where the cost of these changes is "factored" into the selling price, it is very difficult to determine if this factor is adequate. One indication that these factors are not adequate is if revenue is increasing and gross profit margins are decreasing.

What Is the Answer?

While the answer to this problem is difficult, the solution could reside in any of the following:

- Account management needs to point out to the customers the cost of the changes they are asking for. (Especially the next time cost reductions are being negotiated.)
- Manufacturing software needs to be significantly improved to allow for instantaneous updates and access to all the information. From the customer to your company, back to the suppliers, this is a major component of supply-chain management.
- Accounting systems need to track the cost of these customer changes so a determination can be made in terms of who pays for the changes: the suppliers, your company, or the customer. The answer should revolve around who caused or initiated the change and why it was necessary.

FINANCIAL RAMIFICATIONS OF FORECASTING

Forecasting is a process, if you have it documented! All documented processes still contain variation. This variation in the forecasting process is called the *forecast error.*

This variation either has to be accepted, buffered, or a combination of the two. If the level of forecast error is accepted with no buffer, customer service could be potentially impacted in a negative way.

If the decision is to buffer this forecast error with inventory or excess lead-time, the question becomes how much.

To answer the question, you must determine what type of manufacturing environment you have. Different business/manufacturing environments in general have more or less variation in their forecasting/manufacturing process.

The three figures below are depicting the three major types of manufacturing and the amount of deviation one might expect to see in a normal situation. The dotted lines indicate the amount of potential forecast error.

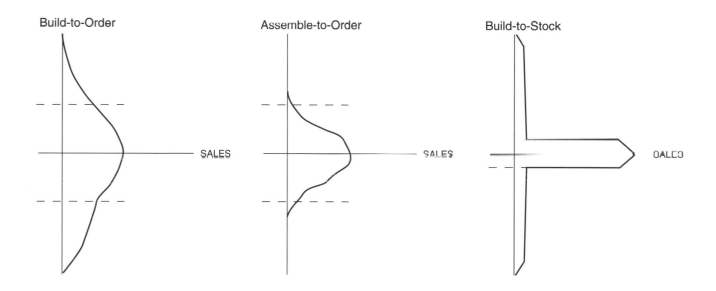

DETERMINING INVENTORY BECAUSE OF FORECAST ERROR

The more accurate your individual product sales forecasting is, the smaller your forecast error, and the less inventory you will have to carry to maintain a specified level of customer service. By carrying less inventory, you can more effectively use the capacity of machines required to build the products. Inventory is not being built before needed, thus not committing capacity of machines too early. By carrying less inventory, less space is used, and it is not used too early.

Since all forecasts have a forecast error, the next question is how to calculate the amount of inventory needed to buffer this forecast error and meet the company's objective of on-time shipment.

One of the most important tools used in determining the required inventory is the *standard deviation of the forecast error* calculation. The purpose of this calculation is to calculate an amount of inventory that will allow for the forecast error and establish a certain probability of still shipping on time.

Standard deviation is a statistical calculation that deals with difference. In the context of this book, it is the difference between forecasted shipments and actual shipments. This difference is called a forecast error. The standard deviation is shown in detail on the next page.

The Role of Safety Stock and Safety Lead-Time

Safety stock is a quantity of stock to keep in inventory to protect against unexpected fluctuations in demand and/or supply. It is usually carried as close to the customer as possible at the finished goods level. However, sometimes it is used to compensate for scrap and obsolete parts. Hard-to-get parts are carried as safety stock to guard against unreliable supplier deliveries.

Safety lead-time—which simply is an inflation of the lead-time—is used sometimes to buffer against customer changes in the original lead-time. Safety lead-time and safety stock have the same effect on inventory; they both create demand for inventory before it is needed. *They both cost money!*

The calculation on the next page shows the steps involved in determining the amount of safety stock for safety lead-time one might consider. This calculation is called the standard deviation of forecast error.

What Causes Inventory Build-Up?

Before proceeding, list as many causes of inventory build-up as you can. See page 76 for a list of potential causes.

_____

_____

_____

_____

_____

_____

_____

_____

_____

PRACTICE: ESSENTIAL CALCULATIONS

STANDARD DEVIATION

Time Periods*	1 Actual Sales	2 Forecast	3 Forecast Error	4 Forecast Error^2 (squared)
1	1520	1510	+10	100
2	1490	1500	-10	100
3	1510	1500	+10	100
4	1520	1500	+20	400
5	1470	1510	-40	1600
6	1510	1500	+10	100
			Total	**2400**

*Time period could be months or years.

Practice: Steps for Calculating Standard Deviation of the Forecast Error

STEP 1 — To calculate forecast error, subtract column 2 from column 1.

STEP 2 — Square each period's forecast error (column 3 x column 3). Remember that when you square a number, you multiply the number by itself.

STEP 3 — Add all the entries/items in column 4. The total equals 2400.

STEP 4 — Calculate the average of the square of the deviation (2400 ÷ 6 periods = 400).

STEP 5 — Now find the square root sign ($\sqrt{\ }$) on your calculator, and determine the square root of 400.

Practice: Answer

The answer you should get is 20, which is the square root of 400. The 20 units equal one positive standard deviation, and if this amount were to be carried in inventory, the probability of on-time shipments would be 84 out of 100 times, or 84% of the time. The answer, 20, is stated as one positive standard deviation. What this means is that if 20 units of inventory were held to buffer against the forecast error, a certain level of on-time shipments would have a probability of happening. Notice how small the inventory level is; this is because of the small forecast error.

For most customers, this would be totally unacceptable, and the supplier would be forced to carry at least two or three positive standard deviations, which would result in doubling or tripling the inventory investment—from 20 units to 40 units or to 60 units. The result would be to increase the number of on-time shipments from 84% to 97.5% to 99.85% of the time (refer to chart below).

Diminishing Returns

Notice that as the inventory doubles and then triples, the on-time shipments increase at a diminishing rate.

Inventory Level	Standard Deviation	Customer Service Level
0	0.00	.50
20	1.00	.84
40	2.00	.975
60	3.00	.9985

Customer Service-Level Table

If you want to ship to customers 100% of the time (99.99967), the inventory would have to be increased six-fold (six positive deviations, also known as 6 sigma) from 20 units to 120 units. Since going from three standard deviations to six will only increase your shipment levels by less than 1%, but require doubling of the inventory from 60 to 120, companies might opt to not ship 100% of the time—just don't tell the customers!

EXERCISE 1

Calculate the standard deviation of the forecast error. Complete the tables below with your calculation. See page 74 for the answers.

Time Period	Forecast	Sales	Forecast Error	Forecast Error^2
1	500	600		
2	500	500		
3	500	400		
4	500	450		
5	500	700		
6	500	600		
7	500	550		
8	500	500		
9	500	350		
10	500	450		
Total	5,000	5,100		

Calculate the standard deviation forecast error.

ANALYZING YOUR CUSTOMERS' FINANCIAL STATEMENTS

Because there has been such wild fluctuations in the forecasts, the Asset Manager has asked you to prepare a report with financial justification that could be presented to the management team to address working together to improve the forecast and forecast error.

For the customer, this presentation will be divided into three parts.

- **Presentation A:** A financial analysis using the information found on pages 67 and 68.
- **Presentation B:** A report to present compelling reasons for why the customer should be interested in helping to reduce the forecast error.
- **Follow-up Presentation:** A report of some financial ramifications using several variables.

PRESENTATION A

CUSTOMER 1: CONSOLIDATED BALANCE SHEETS

($Millions)

	Current Year	Prior Year
ASSETS		
Cash and cash equivalents	179	101
Short-term investments	69	108
Accounts receivable, net	169	210
Inventories	174	197
Other current assets	169	151
Total current assets	760	767
Land, property and equipment, net	583	390
Total Assets	**1,343**	**1,157**
LIABILITIES AND STOCKHOLDERS' EQUITY		
Notes payable	125	135
Accounts payable	45	52
Total current liabilities	170	187
Long-term liabilities	159	100
Total Liabilities	**329**	**287**
Stockholders' equity		
Common stock	458	426
Retained earnings	556	444
Total stockholders' equity	**1,014**	**870**
Total Liabilities and Stockholders' Equity	**$1,343**	**$1,157**

PRESENTATION A (continued)

CUSTOMER 1: CONSOLIDATED STATEMENT OF OPERATIONS

($Millions)

	Current Year	Prior Year
YEAR ENDED		
Net Sales (Revenue)	1,331	1,394
Costs of Goods Sold and Operating Expenses		
Cost of Goods Sold	971	969
Gross Profit	360	425
Sales, general and administrative expenses (SG&A)	215	129
Income from operations	145	296
Interest income	28	18
Income before income taxes	173	314
Provision for income taxes	68	117
Net Income	**105**	**197**

Exercise: Calculate Key Financial Ratios

CUSTOMER 1: CALCULATING RATIOS

1. Using the company's financial statements on the two previous pages, calculate the following ratios (round all decimals back two places). See page 75 for the answers.

Name	Method of Calculation	Current Year	Prior Year
Liquidity Current Ratio	$\dfrac{\text{Current Assets}}{\text{Current Liabilities}}$		
Quick Ratio	$\dfrac{\text{Cash Through Receivables}}{\text{Current Liabilities}}$		
Days Sales Outstanding (DSO)	$\dfrac{\text{Receivables} \times 365}{\text{Net Sales}}$		
Inventory Turnover (Turns)	$\dfrac{\text{Cost of Goods Sold}}{\text{Inventory}}$		
Days' Supply of Inventory	$\dfrac{365 \text{ Days}}{\text{Inventory Turns}}$		
Days' Payables Outstanding	$\dfrac{\text{Payables} \times 365}{\text{Cost of Goods Sold}}$		
Leverage Debt-to-Equity	$\dfrac{\text{Total Liabilities}}{\text{Stockholders' Equity}}$		
Profitability Return on Equity	$\dfrac{\text{Net Income Before Taxes}}{\text{Stockholders' Equity}}$		
Return on Assets	$\dfrac{\text{Net Income Before Taxes}}{\text{Total Assets}}$		

Determination of Cash Flow

Cash flow is either positive or negative; in rare cases it is even. The formula for calculating the cash flow is:

Day's Sales Outstanding (DSO)

+ Day's Supply of Inventory (DSI)

− Day's Payable Outstanding (DPO)

= Positive Cash Flow

(DPS greater than DSO + DSI)

or

= Negative Cash Flow

(DPO less than DSO + DSI)

Cash-to-Cash

DSO = Days' Sales Outstanding

DSI = Days' Supply of Inventory

DPO = Days' Payable Outstanding

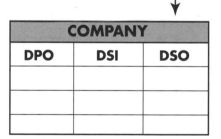

PRESENTATION FOLLOW-UP

See page 77 for the answers.

1. Using the information from Customer 1's financial statements, the Asset Manager has asked you the "dollar impact" of a 50% and a 90% reduction of inventory in terms of *days' supply of inventory and inventory turns*.

Inventory Reduction

Description of Impact	Current year	50% Reduction	90% Reduction
Inventory Turns			
Days' Supply of Inventory			
Net Income Before Taxes			
Return on Assets			
Reduction in Lead-Times			

2. What would be the impact on profit and loss of these reductions, assuming a 30% carrying cost? (Remember carrying includes such things as insurance, taxes, storage, interest on the money to pay for the inventory, and handling costs.)

Description of Impact	Current year	50% Reduction	90% Reduction
Inventory			
Carrying Cost = 30%			
Impact on Net Profit Before Taxes			

What would be the impact on other areas such as:

- Direct Labor: _____

- Quality: _____

- Space and the related occupancy costs: _____

PRESENTATION B

Explain what types of justifications (financial or otherwise) you would present for improving the forecasts and forecast errors. See page 76 for the answers.

Your Company

_____

_____

_____

_____

_____

_____

_____

Customers

_____

_____

_____

_____

Suppliers

_____

_____

_____

_____

_____

_____

_____

_____

REVIEW QUESTIONS

See page 78 for the answers.

1. A customer calls and wants to double their schedule. What would be your action? What would be your concern?

_____

_____

_____

_____

2. The Net Sales and Accounts Receivable are to the Master Schedule what the Cost of Goods Sold is to

   A. Inventory Purchase

   B. Bills of Material

   C. Material Requirements Planning

   D. Accounts Payable

3. The Master Schedule is

   A. Commitment to ship

   B. Commitment of capacity

   C. A plan to schedule the right part at the right time

   D. A and B

4. If the forecast called for shipments of $100 million and the target ending inventory was $5 million dollars, and the beginning inventory was $10 million dollars, the production plan would call for the production of what?

   A. $105 million

   B. $95 million

   C. $96 million

   D. None of the above

5. All of the following are reasons customers might not pay, except

   A. Quality problems with the product

   B. Interpretations of terms and conditions

   C. Letter of credit that has not expired

   D. A and B only

6. The long-term Resource Requirements Plan is to the Production Plan what the critical capacity (bottleneck work-center) is to the

A. MRP

B. Capacity Requirements Plan

C. MPS

D. A and B only

7. The major reason(s) for any type of forecasting is to reconcile the following potentially conflicting objectives:

A. Maximize customer service

B. Maximize efficiency of purchasing

C. Minimize inventory investment

D. Maximize profit

E. All of the above

8. If inventory is released to the shop flow and there is insufficient capacity at the bottleneck work-center, all of the following will increase except

A. Inventory turns

B. Return on Assets

C. Days' supply of inventory

D. Consigned inventory

9. As a quick review, list the impact of excessive lead-times on:

• Return on Assets (ROA):

_____

• Return on Investments (ROI):

_____

• Days' Sales Outstanding (DSO):

_____

• Inventory Turns:

_____

• Days' Supply of Inventory (DSI):

_____

Answers: Exercise 1

Your table should look like the one below.

Time Period	Forecast	Sales	Forecast Error	Forecast Error
1	500	600	100	10,000
2	500	500	0	0
3	500	400	-100	10,000
4	500	450	-50	2,500
5	500	700	200	40,000
6	500	600	100	10,000
7	500	550	50	2,500
8	500	500	0	0
9	500	350	-150	22,500
10	500	450	-50	2,500
Total	**5,000**	**5,100**		**100,000**

ANSWER: Standard Deviation is:

$$\frac{100,000}{10} = 10,000$$

$$\sqrt{10,000} = 100$$

Answers: Calculating Ratios

KEY FINANCIAL RATIOS

(All decimals rounded back two places)

Name	Method of Calculation	Current Year		Prior Year	
Liquidity Current Ratio	$\dfrac{\text{Current Assets}}{\text{Current Liabilities}}$	$\dfrac{760}{170}$	= 4.47	$\dfrac{767}{187}$	= 4.1
Quick Ratio	$\dfrac{\text{Cash Through Receivables}}{\text{Current Liabilities}}$	$\dfrac{179+69+169}{170}$	= 2.45	$\dfrac{101+108+210}{187}$	= 2.24
Days' Sales Outstanding (DSO)	$\dfrac{\text{Receivables} \times 365}{\text{Net Sales}}$	$\dfrac{61,685}{1331}$	= 46	$\dfrac{76,650}{1394}$	= 55
Inventory Turnover	$\dfrac{\text{Cost of Goods Sold}}{\text{Inventory}}$	$\dfrac{971}{174}$	= 5.58	$\dfrac{969}{197}$	= 4.92
Days' Supply of Inventory	$\dfrac{365 \text{ Days}}{\text{Inventory Turns}}$	$\dfrac{365}{5.58}$	= 65	$\dfrac{365}{4.92}$	= 74
Days' Payables Outstanding	$\dfrac{\text{Payables} \times 365}{\text{Cost of Goods Sold}}$	$\dfrac{45 \times 365}{971}$	=16.91	$\dfrac{52 \times 365}{969}$	=19.58
Leverage Debt-to-Equity	$\dfrac{\text{Total Liabilities}}{\text{Stockholders' Equity}}$	$\dfrac{329}{1014}$	= .32	$\dfrac{287}{870}$	= .329
Profitability Return on Equity	$\dfrac{\text{Net Income Before Taxes}}{\text{Stockholders' Equity}}$	$\dfrac{173}{1014}$	= .17	$\dfrac{314}{870}$	= .36
Return on Assets	$\dfrac{\text{Net Income Before Taxes}}{\text{Total Assets}}$	$\dfrac{173}{1343}$	= .13	$\dfrac{314}{1157}$	= .27

Answers: Presentation B

Your Company

1. Fewer obsolete and excess material charges on changes, especially end of life.
2. Less "fire sale" of low-margin business to get rid of excess and obsolete inventory.
3. Shorter lead-times, less inventory tied up.
4. Better utilization of capacity.
5. Proactive utilization of team members (customer focus/satisfaction team).
6. Increased quality levels by having a more consistent workforce.
7. Increased profitability by lowering the material inventory at both the company and the suppliers.
8. Decreased expediting and cancellation charges passed on from the supplier.
9. Less exposures on ECOs (scrap, rework, material overhead, field inventory, and so on).
10. Opportunity to reduce frozen time fences, thus increasing flexibility.
11. Improved cash flow.
12. More accurate forecast, reduced safety stock inventory, thus increasing inventory turns and ROA, and decreasing days' supply of inventory and current liabilities (accounts payable for material purchases).
13. Decrease manufacturing lead-time (queue, wait, move, and set-up) thus reducing inventory with the same results as mentioned in number 12.
14. Reduce the need for cash on hand, therefore increasing the quick ratio.

Customers

1. Increased commitment to ship-date performance.
2. Less "fire sale" of low margin business to get rid of excess and obsolete inventory.
3. Shorter lead-times in terms of delivery dates.
4. Less exposure on Engineering Change Orders (ECOs) (scrap, rework, and material overhead for products shipped to their customer).

Suppliers

1. Combination of all of the above.

What Causes Inventory Build-Up?
Answers

- No contract, poorly written or executed contract
- Inaccurate customer forecast
- Changes to customer forecast
- ECOs
- Minimum order quantity
- Supplier missed delivery
- Acquisitions
- Project on hold

- Supplier's terms & conditions different from customer's
- Materials shortages
- Safety stock
- Human buffering (expanded lot sizes)
- Quality issue
- Excess & obsolete inventory
- Inaccurate BOM

Answers: Follow-Up

A. Did you get these answers?

Inventory Reduction

Inventory Turns	05.58	$\frac{971}{87}$ =11.16	$\frac{971}{17.4}$ = 55.80
Days' Supply of Inventory	65.00	32.50	$\frac{365}{55.8}$ = 06.50
Net Income Before Taxes	173.00	↑ * 26 to $199	↑ 47 to $220
Return on Assets Before Taxes	.13	$\frac{199}{1343}$ = .15	$\frac{220}{1343}$ = .16
Reduction in Lead-Times	N/A	50%	90%

B. The impact on the net income of these reductions, assuming a 30% carrying cost is as follows. Remember, carrying costs include such things as insurance, taxes, storage, and so on.

Inventory	$174	87.00	174 – 17.40 = 156.60
Carrying Costs = 30%	30% x 174 = 52.20	30% x 87 = 26.10 ↓	30% x 156.6 = 46.98 ↓
Impact on Net Income Before Taxes		*26 ↑ (rounded)	*47 ↑ (rounded)

(*This is a one-time only savings.)

C. The impact on other areas would include:
*   Direct Labor: *1) Would not be committed to inventory too early. 2) Could be used in other areas that are under-capacity. 3) More flexibility to respond to customer changes*
*   Quality: *1) Would potentially improve because smaller lot sizes would reduce the amount of inventory that would be subject to defects if they did happen*
*   Space and the related occupancy costs: *1) Would decrease because the inventory would not be built before it was needed and materials would not be bought before required*

Answers: Review

1. A customer calls and wants to double their schedule. What would your action be? What would be your concern?

ACTIONS

Meet with the team to decide what to do

Check MRP to see what's on order

Work over-time

Determine validity or order

Review labor capacities with management, get approved for over-time

Suggest engineer involvement

ESCALATE IF ISSUES ARE UNANSWERED

CONCERNS

Price negotiation (increases, decreases, economies of scale)?

Consigned Material, or KIT, lets the customer finish part of the product

What-if reports, is there enough capacity?

Is it a new product?

Is BOM current?

Delivery schedule, partials? Start time?

Capacity (material availability, labor, training curve)?

Can we hire (freeze trained personnel)?

Process changes, Engineering Change Orders (ECOs), and related expedite fees?

Test and yield (Is it possible? How will it be affected?) Quality: (How it is affected?)

2. C
3. D
4. B (100 + 5 –10 = 95)
5. C
6. C
7. E
8. B
9. ROA goes down; ROI goes down; DSO might or might not have an impact; Inventory turns goes down; DSI goes up

IV

TYING FINANCIAL INFORMATION TO MANUFACTURING INFORMATION

LEARNING OBJECTIVES

After completing this chapter, you will be able to:

- Compute a basic manufacturing formula

- List the impact on assets of three different business plan scenarios

- Explain key terms and definitions

- Calculate capacity and explain its impact on asset management

- Show the financial ramifications of MRP

RECONCILING THE PHYSICAL FLOW WITH THE FINANCIAL INFORMATION FLOW

In this chapter, you will continue "pulling together" your presentation. In this part, one of your primary objectives is to sell to your internal customers the financial benefits of reducing inventory and improving the MRP. The results will be an improvement of asset management throughout the closed-loop MRPII process.

- The "tie-in" of the manufacturing systems with the financial systems continues. The Material Requirement Plan (MRP), Bills of Material (BOM), and lead-time will be tied to costs such as direct material, direct labor, and overhead.
- The cost of changes to BOMs specifically as they relate to engineering changes, and inaccurate/ incomplete BOMs will be shown.
- The cost related to incomplete routings and over-and-under lead-times will be calculated.
- Finally, a financial analysis of a theoretical company called "YOUR COMPANY" will be completed.

To begin with, let's look at the theory behind MRP and the basic concepts of the Bills of Material:

THE BASIC ACCOUNTING/MANUFACTURING FORMULA

Basic Accounting / Manufacturing Formula		Units	Dollars (millions)
	Beginning inventory	1,000	1,000
+	Production levels (build plan)	9,500	9,500
=	Available inventory to ship (at cost)	10,500	10,500
–	Shipments/Sales (cost of goods sold)	10,000	10,000
=	Ending inventory	500	500

One of the major challenges in companies today is reconciling the financial information flow with the manufacturing (from MPS through MRP and on to the suppliers) with the physical flow of the parts from suppliers into manufacturing and then on to the customers.

In many cases, products can actually be built faster than orders can be entered and processed through the manufacturing and purchasing information systems. In many companies, information systems bottlenecks have taken the place of manufacturing (machine) bottlenecks.

MATERIAL REQUIREMENTS PLANNING

Once the demand from the forecast and customer orders is matched with the supply from production and suppliers, the Master Schedule is ready to be exploded into the Material Requirements Plan. From a financial standpoint, purchase orders are sent to suppliers, who in turn ship the required inventory, thus creating Accounts Payable, which in turn are paid for out of the cash on the Balance Sheet. At this point inventory starts tying up cash that will not be offset with cash collections from Accounts Receivable until the customer receives the final products and pays for them. (A description of Material Requirements Planning is presented later in this chapter.)

Reducing Days' Supply of Inventory by Reducing Lead-Time

The exhibit below further shows the relationship between return on assets (ROA), inventory, inventory turns, days' supply of inventory, and lead-time:

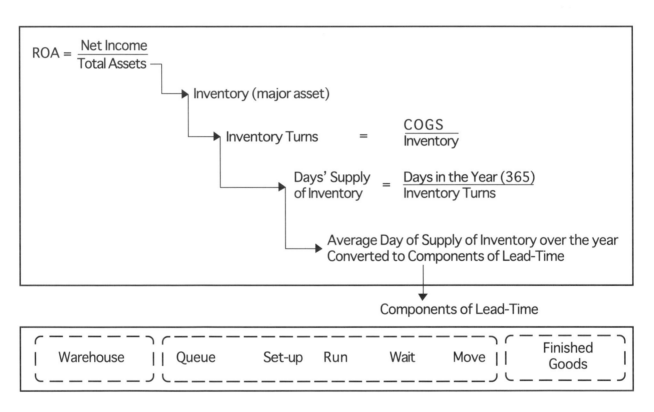

What happens to quality when days' supply of inventory goes down? _____

What other costs go down when days' supply of inventory goes down? _____

It's easy to see how the forecast error can impact not only inventory but inventory turns and days' supply of inventory as well.

Inventory Turns and Days of Supply

As mentioned earlier, one measure of how quickly the inventory is moving through the facilities is a calculation called inventory turns. The calculation is made as follows:

$$\text{Inventory Turns} = \frac{\text{Cost of Goods Sold (Income Statement)}}{\text{Inventory (Balance Sheet)}}$$

To demonstrate this calculation, let's assume the following:

$$\frac{\text{Cost of Goods Sold}}{\text{Inventory}} \quad \frac{\$35 \text{ Million}}{\$5 \text{ Million}}$$

On the surface, seven turns would be very good, especially if your company operates at only two or three turns.

However, upon further examination, seven turns means that inventory (on average) is moving from the Balance Sheet to the Income Statement seven times. This also means at any one time, there is 52 days' worth of inventory sitting within the company.

365 days ÷ 7 inventory turns = 52 days of supply inventory

Fifty-two days' worth of inventory has a very negative impact on the cash flow of the business, especially because the maximum one can build and ship is one day's (24 hours) worth of inventory. Another way of looking at this example is that there are 50+ days' worth of inventory sitting somewhere in the facility with absolutely no value being added.

Taking this example one step further, and assuming the Accounts Payable terms and the Accounts Receivable terms are both 30 days, these 50+ days' supply of inventory would have a very negative impact on cash flow.

Lead-Time

One can further analyze this 50+ days' supply of inventory by analyzing lead-time. The major components of lead-time are:

- QUEUE (inventory sitting on the shop floor or in the warehouse)
- SET-UP (the time preparing machinery and people to do work)
- RUN (the actual work itself)
- WAIT (waiting for cool down, or just to move the parts to the next work center)
- MOVE (the time it takes to actually move the item to the next work center or finished goods)

Since RUN is the only value-added element of lead-time, and the maximum time you can run in a day is 24 hours (assuming three shifts), it still leaves a large proportion of that 50+ days' supply of inventory with absolutely nothing going on, with no value being added whatsoever.

The longer the inventory sits prior to shipment, the more opportunity for customer changes, which could cause rework to inventory already complete.

The more days' supply of inventory, the more people and machine capacity used before actually needed. The result is less flexibility.

The longer the manufacturing lead-time:

- The more inventory there will be on the Balance Sheet, and the lower the ROA will be.
- The more cash there is tied up in inventory that will potentially be written off as obsolete. This will result in a lower ROA as well as a lower ROI.
- The more cash there is tied up inventory, the less cash there is available for such critical functions such as new product development or new acquisitions.
- The more inventory there is that will potentially be worked on before it needs to be, thus using the capacity of the machine and/or person before the time needed. This also reduces flexibility by committing this capacity too early and then not being able to react to changes on a real-time basis.

REDUCING INVENTORY WITH "BETTER INFORMATION"

As can be seen, inventory is a very expensive asset. The major objective of every company should be to replace this expensive asset with another asset called information. However, in order to do this, the information about the inventory must be accurate, reliable, consistent, and timely.

Let's look now at how this might happen by reflecting again on the components of lead-time (queue, set-up, run, wait, and move) and our example where there were seven turns ($35M /$5M = 7), and the 52 days' supply of inventory.

In this example, a very good case could be made that 90% or more of this lead-time was in non-value-added areas, and 10% of the time would be the actual run.

Simply not buying or issuing inventory before it was needed (remember there are 52 days of inventory) could achieve this reduction of 90% in inventory. Many companies readily agree that upon reflection this non-value-added time is anywhere between 70% and 90%. The exception is those companies whose inventory turns are in the high 20s. Remember, many companies who profess to be JIT or demand pull are happy to have turns of 12 or less, which still says there is 30 days or more worth of inventory, not only on the Balance Sheet, but physically sitting somewhere in the company.

Even if you do have 12 turns, you have neither a positive nor a negative cash-flow effect, assuming once again our example of 30 days for Accounts Payable and Accounts Receivable.

Creating the Vision

Let's create a vision for a moment and see what the impact of this 90% reduction in queue or the other non-value-added parts of lead-time would be.

Original example:

$$\frac{\text{Cost of Goods Sold}}{\text{Inventory}} = \frac{\$35 \text{ Million}}{\$5 \text{ Million}} = 7$$

- Ninety percent reduction in inventory would equal a $4,460,000 reduction in inventory.
- The turns would be 7 and the days' supply of inventory would be a little over 5.
- This decrease in inventory would also have a very dramatic impact on the ROA calculation.
- The cash flow in this example will be a positive 25 days (assuming once again our example of 30 days to pay and 30 days in which to get paid).
- Inventory build-up, while extremely costly, might not be the biggest cost. The biggest cost might turn out to be the cost of customer changes.

FINANCIAL IMPACT OF CUSTOMERS CHANGING THEIR MIND

The situation described in the prior pages regarding inventory turns can worsen when unexpected changes occur, especially customer changes. Many marketing people, financial people, and executives have little appreciation for the time the entire process takes. It takes time to analyze and make corrections or changes, not just to the customer order, but all the way through manufacturing process and outward to the affected suppliers.

Additional time and considerable talent in negotiating must be used with the suppliers and the operations people to make changes.

This situation causes a large number of part shortages and late deliveries, both from suppliers and to customers. In addition, costs such as premiums and expedite charges are incurred, which seldom get passed on to the customer.

The cost of customer changes result in premiums, expedite fees, engineering change orders (ECOs), and obsolete inventory charges. If these are paid by the company and not passed back to the customer, the result is an erosion of the profit margin. These additional examples of the hidden cost of manufacturing are never fully analyzed because most, if not all, accounting software does not track these costs. This is because they end up as purchase-price variances, or in cases where cost of Engineering Change Orders (ECOs) are not calculated, as inventory write-offs not charged to the customer who causes them.

Time Lost in the Product Life Cycle

Another growing cost of customer changes is the cost of time lost in the product life cycle, and not just the company's, but the customer's as well. Many times customers have much shorter life cycles, and yet they make changes up until the very last minute before shipment, which postpones the delivery of the product. In addition, these changes cause quality problems, which take even more time and impact cash flow in a very negative way.

Many Manufacturing Professionals Have Little Appreciation for the Time and Cost Required to Make Changes

EXERCISE 1

In the space provided below, list at least five financial ramifications of having inventory sitting with absolutely no value being added.

_____

_____

_____

_____

_____

MANUFACTURING RESOURCE PLANNING/MRPII

Let's look again at the closed-loop MRPII/ERP system and discuss the tie-in of COGS to MRP, BOMs, and lead-time.

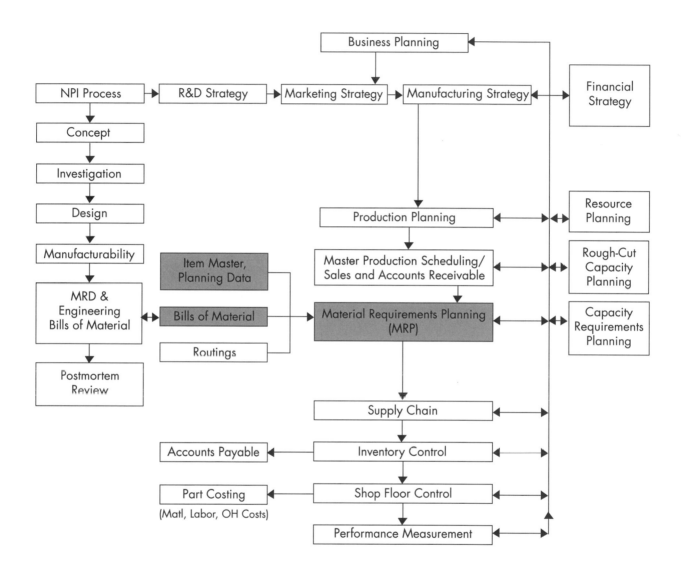

A horizontal, time-sensitive representation would look like the following:

R&D		and	Manufacturing Lead-Time
Supplier Environment		and	Lead-Times
Customer's Environment		and	Their Customers

MATERIAL REQUIREMENTS PLANNING

Once the demand from the forecast and customer orders is matched with the supply from production and suppliers, the Master Schedule is ready to be exploded into the Material Requirement Plan. From a financial standpoint, purchase orders are sent to suppliers, who in turn ship the required inventory, thus creating Accounts Payable, which in turn are paid for out of the cash on the Balance Sheet. At this point inventory starts tying up cash that will not be offset with cash collections from Accounts Receivable until the customer receives the final products and pays for them.

Material Requirements Planning (MRP) uses information from the Master Production Schedule (MPS) to schedule the right part, at the right time, to the right place. The MRP suggests what to release, reprioritizes orders, and generates reports that make suggestions for the cycle counts. MRP also provides data to support priority planning and capacity requirements planning, as well as scheduling, dispatching, and purchasing systems. From a financial standpoint, MRP represents inventory and Accounts Payable.

MRP is driven by input from the MPS. The product of the MPS is derived primarily from the forecast, customer orders, spare part and service requirements, interdivisional orders, new product requirements, and perhaps even special marketing promotions. If an item is not included in the Master Schedule, the parts needed to build it cannot be scheduled by the MRP.

The MRP schedules requirements for all component parts. These are combined to develop the gross requirements for each part. An MRP system suggests inventory levels over a specified period of time, order policies, bills or material explosions, and the time-phased planning of the release of material to built on the shop floor or to be purchased from suppliers and contractors.

The reports generated by MRP provide decision-making tools for the placement and rescheduling of manufacturing orders and purchase orders.

Implement Material Requirements Planning

MRP addresses the nature of demand and determines how planned material supply will satisfy that demand. Planning for material includes generating net requirements and maintaining priorities.

The term *component item* in MRP covers the scheduling of all parts required to make the end items called for by the MPS. Component items can include raw material, semi-finished and piece parts, subassemblies and so on. The Master Schedule (independent demand) creates the dependent demand from a BOM, which lists the parts and quantities required to build each item, and explodes into the MRP.

A subassembly or component is a raw material, ingredient, or part used at a higher level to make up an assembly. Subassemblies or components include everything that is part of MRP.

CREATE A BILL OF MATERIAL

When there is demand for an end item, and you've decided to build it, you will need to schedule material by following the MRP process.

Parent/Component Relationship: Structuring the BOM

A BOM contains a list of parts and quantities required to build an end-item. The establishment of the relationship between the end-item and its parts, called *structuring the BOM*, is done systematically through a process of establishing the parent-component relationship.

BOM structuring is the process that organizes BOMs and results in the subassemblies that go into assemblies and then becomes part of the end-product. Each parent-component relationship establishes links between the end-item and its parts or between two or more parts. The graphic on the next page shows a BOM structure with parent and components.

PARENT STRUCTURE LEVELS

Every part in a product structure is given a code indicating the level in which that part is used within the BOM. It is a common practice to designate the end-item/product as level 0. The subsequent assemblies, subassemblies, and raw materials are assigned levels 1, 2, and so on down through the product structure. The MRP system uses this product structure to explode downward, level by level. The lowest level in which an item is structured in the BOM is called the low-level code. The MRP logic requires the establishment of the low-level code when it is calculating part requirements.

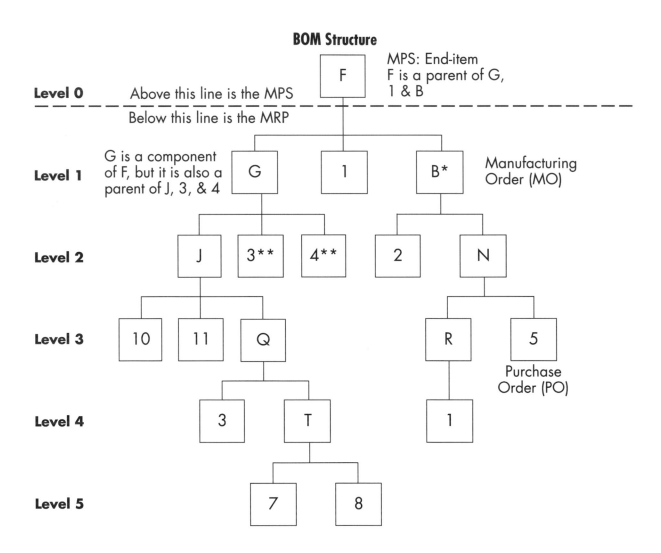

* A manufacturing order (work order) would be required to build part B as well as to any other "alpha" character.

** A purchase order would be needed to acquire parts 3 and 4, as well as to any other numeric part number. As a rule of thumb, whenever there are no components to the part, a purchase order is required.

Note: For purposes of this book, subassemblies or any component built internally will have part numbers that begin with alphabetical characters. Purchase part numbers will begin with numerical characters.

THE COSTED BILL OF MATERIAL

A costed bill of material is a bill of material that has been expanded to include the standard costs for direct material, direct labor, and factory overhead.

- Direct material is defined as the material that goes directly into the product that is being built.
- Direct labor is the labor cost and time involved in actually building—putting all the parts together to create the salable product.
- Overhead is all other manufacturing-related costs, indirect material (oils, lubricants, and so on) and indirect labor (supervision, purchasing, MIS, and so on). Another way of looking at overhead is that it includes all other costs except direct materials and direct labor.

Direct material, direct labor, and factory overhead make up the vast majority of the inventory value that, when sold, becomes the cost of goods sold (COGs).

The accuracy of the costed bill of material is essential in setting the sale price and margins when pricing a new product.

Establishing the Sales Price/Net Sales

Correct calculations of the selling price to the customer is of great importance. Impact to the profit will be affected if the incorrect calculation is used.

Retailers and wholesalers typically use a *mark-up,* consequently, most consumers are more familiar with this methodology. Many manufacturers use the *margin* model. In a manufacturing environment, the selling price should always be calculated using the margin formula.

Margin and Markup Calculations

The example below shows the difference in selling price when using the two types of calculations.

Example: Margin % Calculation	Example: Mark-up % Calculation
	(not to be used to calculate selling price)
Unit Cost = $400	Unit Cost = $400
Margin = 20%	Mark-up = 20%
$$\frac{400}{1-\text{margin } \%}$$	Cost $\times$ (1 + mark-up %)
Selling price using the margin calculation:	Selling price using the mark-up % calculation:
$\dfrac{400}{1-.20}$ or $.80$ = $500.00	400 $\times$ 1.20 = $480.00

EXPLANATION OF COST BUILD-UP

Starting at Level 2 , there are parts #3 and #4, with a purchased cost of $4 and $6, respectively. When parts #3 and #4 are delivered to a work center, direct labor is charged at a stated cost of one hour at $15 per hour. Factory overhead is added at a standard cost of $30 per labor hour. The total cost of subassembly G is $89 ($20 for part #3, $24 for part #4, $15 for direct labor, and $30 for factory overhead).

The cost build-up continues by combining part #1 with subassembly G, which would result in product F and a total cost of $242 ($89 for subassembly G, $9 material costs for part #1, and $36 direct labor x 3 hours equals $108 of factory overhead).

In summary, Direct Labor is the labor costs involved by those actually putting the product together; Factory Overhead includes all the other costs—salaries of purchasing, information services people, managers, depreciation and other.

Bills of Material

Following is an explanation of the process of how the various components involved in the manufacturing process (component price, labor, and factory overhead) impact the final selling price of a part or end item.

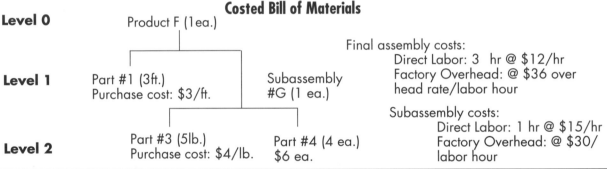

Costed Bill of Materials

Level 0 — Product F (1ea.)

Level 1 — Part #1 (3ft.) Purchase cost: $3/ft.   Subassembly #G (1 ea.)

Final assembly costs:
Direct Labor: 3 hr @ $12/hr
Factory Overhead: @ $36 overhead rate/labor hour

Level 2 — Part #3 (5lb.) Purchase cost: $4/lb.   Part #4 (4 ea.) $6 ea.

Subassembly costs:
Direct Labor: 1 hr @ $15/hr
Factory Overhead: @ $30/labor hour

Part #	Material $	Labor $	Overhead $	Total $
Subassembly G: From Part #3: 5 lb x $4/lb	20			20
From Part #4: 4 ea x $6 ea	24			24
Labor: 1 hr x $15/hr		15		15
Overhead: 1 hr x $30/hr			30	30
Subtotal of G	**44**	**15**	**30**	**89**
Final Assembly F costs:				
From Part #1: 3 ft x $3/ft	9			9
From Subassembly G;	44	15	30	89
Labor to assembly F: 3 hr x $12/hr		36		36
Overhead to assemble F: 3 hr x $36/hr			108	108
Total end item F costs:	**53**	**51**	**138**	**242**

DETERMINE GROSS-TO-NET REQUIREMENTS

The MPS uses the information contained in a BOM to create the MRP explosion. The term explosion in this context means going from one level to the next in the BOM (such as level 0 to level 1).

The following figure shows a simplified sequence that the Master Schedule and MRP would follow in order to translate independent demand into dependent demand. Each of these terms is discussed in detail below.

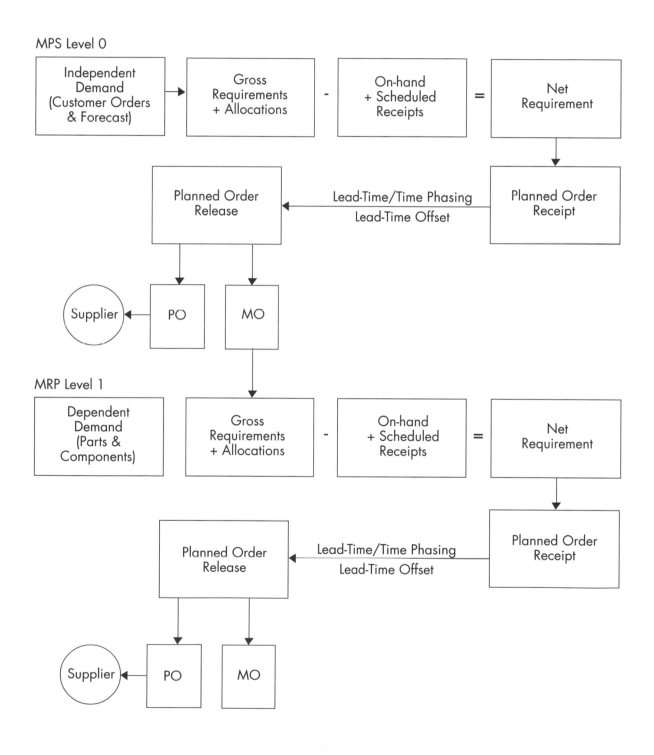

Process for Determining Gross-to-Net Requirements

Independent Demand—Independent demand comes from sources such as the forecast, customer orders for end-items and repair parts, and orders from other divisions of your company. Independent demand is demand for an end-item or service part that is unrelated to the demand for other items. The MPS contains only independent demand.

Gross Requirements—Gross requirements are the total dependent and/or independent requirements for a product or part prior to accounting for the item currently on hand or scheduled to be received.

Allocations—The allocation process reserves for manufacturing orders parts that have not been released to the shop floor from the warehouse. An allocation creates a picking list that goes to the warehouse. The allocated part might not be sent from the warehouse until later, so an allocation ensures that the part will not be used to fill another order.

On-hand Inventory—On-hand inventory is the quantity that is physically located in stock, shown in the inventory records as being physically in stock. Periodically, this on-hand inventory is reconciled to the financial inventory (book inventory).

Scheduled Receipts—Scheduled receipts are orders already released (opened) either to manufacturing (production, manufacturing, or shop orders), or to suppliers. Receipts released in a prior planning period are scheduled to arrive during the subsequent planning.

Net Requirements—The net requirements are order amounts that remain after one subtracts on-hand and scheduled receipts from gross requirements and allocations.

MRP Computer Logic Flow

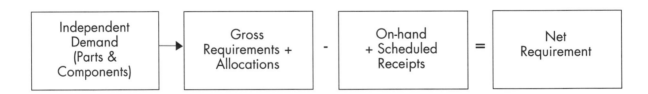

DETERMINE GROSS-TO-NET REQUIREMENTS

(continued)

Planned Order Receipt—When there is a net requirement, you must plan to receive an order to satisfy it. If you do not, a material shortage will result. A planned order receipt is the quantity you plan to receive at a future date. Planned order receipts differ from scheduled receipts in that they might change during subsequent planning periods. Scheduled receipts, on the other hand, have been built or are in the process of being built, either by suppliers or internally. Changes to the scheduled receipts are very costly.

Lead-Time—In order to receive an order, you need to determine the amount of time it takes to receive the order from your manufacturing floor or from the supplier. This length of time is called lead-time. The major components of lead-time are *queue* (the time the inventory is sitting on the shop floor waiting to be worked on), *set-up* (time spent preparing the machine), *run time* (time the machine is actually running), *wait* (time for the item to be moved to the next machine) and *move time.* (The actual movement to the next machine, finished goods inventory, or the end customer.)

Time Phasing/Lead-Time Offsetting—Time phasing enables you to look into the future in order to plan.

This lead-time offset is established by determining when the part is needed to satisfy a requirement. This allows the MRP system to schedule a planned order receipt in one time period and the planned order release in an earlier time period. The difference between these two dates is the required lead-time to make or buy.

Planned Order Release—Creates either a purchase order that is sent to the supplier or a manufacturing order that creates a gross requirement at the next level, Level 1.

Once either the purchase order or the manufacturing order is released, it becomes a scheduled receipt.

MRP Computer Logic Flow (continued)

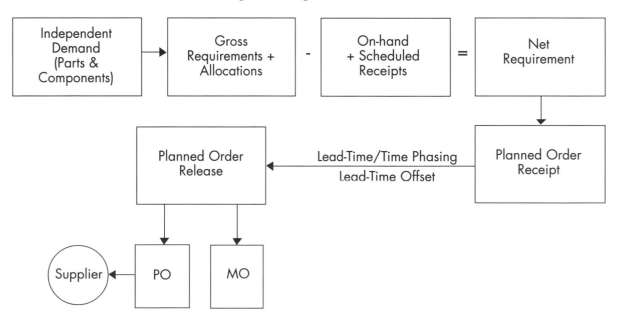

Planned Order Release—A planned order release suggests that an order be created, including quantity, release date, and due date. It suggests that a purchase order (PO) or manufacturing order (MO) is to be created. Planned orders exist only within the MRP system and might be changed or deleted by the computer during subsequent MRP processing if conditions change.

The planned order release results in purchase orders, which are given to suppliers, and manufacturing orders, which are sent to the shop floor. In the case of an MO, a planned order release at one level creates a gross requirement at the next level. When you open an MO, you release it to the manufacturing floor. An MO is a document, group of documents, or schedule conveying authority for the manufacture of specified parts or products in specified quantities.

MRP Computer Logic Flow (continued)

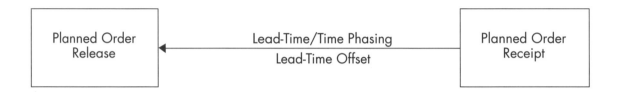

Dependent Demand—Dependent Demand is the demand for all the components required to satisfy the dependent or independent demand from a higher level.

Dependent demand is directly related to or derived from the BOM structure for other components or end-products. These demands are calculated, not forecasted. Independent demand is forecasted, and any given item might have both dependent and independent demand. For example, a part might be the component of an assembly, and also be sold as a service part. The MRP represents dependent demand.

MRP Computer Logic Flow (continued)

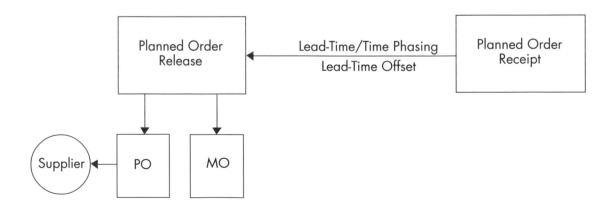

Exercise 2 - *Addendum*

In this exercise you are going to build on what you've just read by doing a complete MRP calculation for product F and its components. See page 109 for the answers.

Planning period = 6 periods

Level 0 Product F	Master Schedule Independent Demand	Week					
		1	2	3	4	5	6
	Gross Requirements	150	100	200	50	150	500
	Scheduled Receipts	250					
Lot size = 400	Projected On Hand = 250						
Lead-time	Net Requirements						
Offset = 3 weeks	Planned Order Receipts						
	Planned Order Release						

	MRP Calculations for Product F	Week					
		1	2	3	4	5	6
Level 1 Part G	Gross Requirements						
	Scheduled Receipts						
	On-hand = 250						
Lot size = 350	Net Requirement(s)						
Lead-time	Planned Order Receipt						
Offset = 1 week	Planned Order Release						

	MRP Calculations for Product F	Week					
		1	2	3	4	5	6
Level 2 Part J	Gross Requirements						
	Scheduled Receipts						
	On-hand = 350						
Lot size = 600	Net Requirement(s)						
Lead-time	Planned Order Receipt						
Offset = 1 week	Planned Order Release						

	MRP Calculations for Product F	Week					
		1	2	3	4	5	6
Level 3 Part 10	Gross Requirements						
	Scheduled Receipts		1000				
	On-hand = 750						
Lot size = 1000	Net Requirement(s)						
Lead-time	Planned Order Receipt						
Offset = 6 weeks	Planned Order Release						

The 1000 units were released in a prior planning period.

Ramifications of Incorrect BOM Structuring

Once an understanding of how MRP logic works, the importance of three key items becomes even more important.

- Item #1 A bill of material (BOM) that is 100% accurate

- Item #2 A routing that is (100%) complete

- Item #3 Lead-times that reflect how much time it *really* takes from the time the material enters the "building" (becomes an Accounts Payable) until it leaves (becomes an Accounts Receivable)

The ramification of not developing a BOM that is 100% correct as soon as possible is tremendous.

Routing

The document that describes where on the shop floor the material needs to be sent is called a *routing*. (In the following scenario, if you take the bill of material and turn it on its side you have a routing.)

A routing is a set of information detailing the method of manufacture of a particular item. It includes the operations to be performed, their sequence, the various work centers to be involved, and the standards for set-up and run. In some companies, the routing also includes information on tooling, operator skill levels, inspection operations, and testing requirements.

The following exhibits show different scenarios.

- Scenario A: A situation where a new part was not included in the bill of material.

- Scenario B: A situation where the routing was never defined or was not included in the bill of material.

- Scenario C: A situation where the lead-times are incorrect.

EXERCISE 3

To reinforce the impact of various manufacturing errors and their impact, a series of scenarios have been presented in the following pages. The Asset Manager has asked you to complete these following exercises related to these scenarios to be used later in your final presentation. See page 110 for the answers.

Scenario A: Part Was Not Included in the BOM

A BOM contains missing part 1 (it was never included in the structuring of the initial bill of material). After looking at each of the scenarios below, answer the questions on the next page.

PRODUCT STRUCTURE TREE—The product structure as mentioned earlier, is a list of parts and quantities "per" that go into the end items. Part 1 is the missing part.

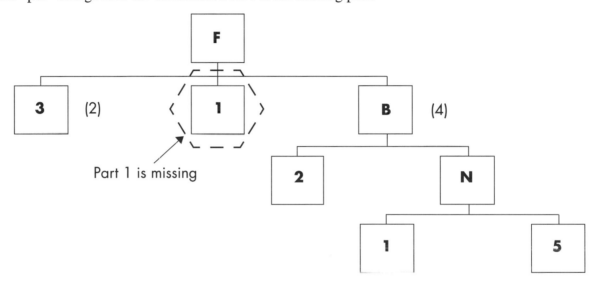

Scenario B: Lead-Time Does Not Include the Time to Purchase Part 1

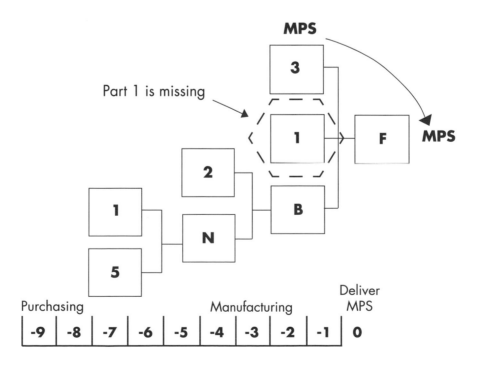

Scenario C: Part 1 Not Structured to Routing

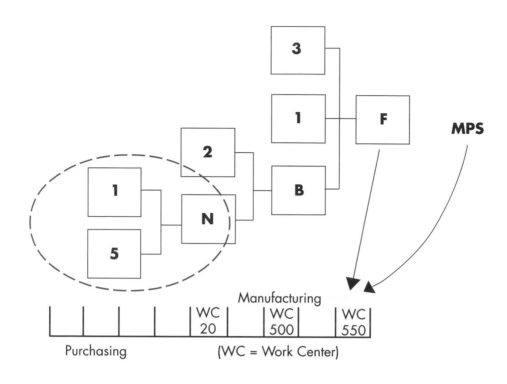

What are the impacts of the previous three scenarios on:

Financial (Profitability) _____

_____

Customer Satisfaction _____

_____

Productivity _____

_____

Inventory _____

_____

CONSOLIDATED BALANCE SHEET—YOUR COMPANY #1

($Millions)

Year ended	Current Year	Prior Year
ASSETS		
Current assets:		
Cash and equivalents	225	228
Short-term investments	257	181
Accounts receivable	416	339
Inventories	494	368
Prepaid expenses and other current assets	79	24
Total current assets	**1,471**	**1,140**
Net property and equipment	379	306
Total assets	**1,850**	**1,446**
LIABILITIES AND STOCKHOLDERS' EQUITY		
Current liabilities:		
Accounts payable	416	294
Other current liabilities	125	60
Total current liabilities	541	354
Long-term debt	388	391
Total liabilities	**929**	**745**
STOCKHOLDERS' EQUITY		
Paid-in capital	443	379
Retained earnings	478	322
Total stockholders' equity	**921**	**701**
Total Liabilities and Stockholders' Equity	**1,850**	**1,446**

CONSOLIDATED INCOME STATEMENT

($Millions)

	Current Year	Prior Year
Year ended		
Net Sales (Revenue)	**3,694**	**2,817**
Cost of sales	**3,266**	**2,534**
Gross profit	**428**	**283**
OPERATING EXPENSES		
Selling, general and administrative	172	100
Research and development	20	7
Total operating expenses	**192**	**107**
Operating income	236	176
Interest income	28	13
Interest expenses	(26)	(15)
Income before income taxes	**238**	**174**
Income taxes	**80**	**58**
Net Income	**158**	**116**

EXERCISE 4

Using the company's financial statements on pages 101 and 102, calculate the following ratios (round all decimals back two places). See page 110 for the answers.

Key Financial Ratios

Name	Method of Calculation	Current Year	Prior Year
Liquidity Current Ratio	$\dfrac{\text{Current Assets}}{\text{Current Liabilities}}$		
Quick Ratio	$\dfrac{\text{Cash Through Receivables}}{\text{Current Liabilities}}$		
Day's Sales Outstanding (DSO)	$\dfrac{\text{Receivables} \times 365}{\text{Net Sales}}$		
Inventory Turnover (Turns)	$\dfrac{\text{Cost of Goods Sold}}{\text{Inventory}}$		
Days' Supply of Inventory	$\dfrac{365 \text{ Days}}{\text{Inventory Turns}}$		
Days' Payables Outstand (DPO)	$\dfrac{365 \text{ Days} \times 365}{\text{Cost of Goods Sold}}$		
Leverage Debt-to-Equity	$\dfrac{\text{Total Liabilities}}{\text{Stockholders' Equity}}$		
Profitability Return on Equity	$\dfrac{\text{Net Income Before Taxes}}{\text{Stockholders' Equity}}$		
Return on Assets	$\dfrac{\text{Net Income Before Taxes}}{\text{Total Assets}}$		

EXERCISE 5

PART 1: Using the information from YOUR COMPANY'S financial statements, the Asset Manager has asked you to calculate the "dollarized" impact of a 50% and a 90% reduction of inventory in terms of days' supply of inventory and inventory turns. See page 111 for the answers.

Inventory Reduction

Description of Impact	Current year	50% Reduction	90% Reduction
Inventory Turns			
Days' Supply of Inventory			
Net Income Before Taxes			
Return on Assets			
Reduction in Lead-Times			

PART II—What would be the impact on profit and loss of these reductions, assuming a 30% carrying cost? (Remember carrying includes such things as insurance, taxes, storage, interest on the money to pay for the inventory and handling costs.)

Description of Impact	Current year	50% Reduction	90% Reduction
Inventory			
Carrying Cost = 30%			
Impact on Net Profit			

What would be the impact on other areas, such as:

- Direct Labor:_____

  _____

- Quality: _____

  _____

- Space and the related occupancy costs: _____

  _____

- Indirect Labor: _____

  _____

REVIEW QUESTIONS

See page 112 for the answers.

1. The major reason for managing assets includes all of the following except:

    A. Maximize inventory

    B. Maximize customer service

    C. Maximize the efficiency of purchasing and production

    D. Maximize profit

2. Following is the formula for ROI:

    A. $$\frac{\text{Net Profit}}{\text{Stockholders' Equity}}$$

    B. $$\frac{\text{Assets}}{\text{Stockholders' Equity}}$$

    C. $$\frac{\text{Cost of Goods Sold}}{\text{Average Sales}}$$

    D. $$\frac{\text{Net Loss}}{\text{Stockholders' Equity}}$$

3. In lead-time, the only value-added item is?

    A. Queue time

    B. Wait time

    C. Run time

    D. Run time and set-up time

4. Assuming the maximum amount that can be shipped at any one time is one days' worth of capacity of the bottleneck work center, the amount of excess inventory (non-value added) for a company with ten inventory turns would be what?

    A. 100 days

    B. 10 days

    C. Both A and B

    D. None of the above

5. If lead-time is incorrect, which of the following will be impacted?

    A. Financial results

    B. Productivity of the people

    C. The number of engineering change orders will increase

    D. A and C only

    E. A and B only

6. According to the BOM structure below,

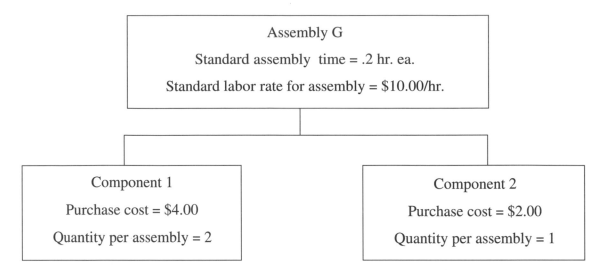

Assembly G

Standard assembly time = .2 hr. ea.

Standard labor rate for assembly = $10.00/hr.

Component 1

Purchase cost = $4.00

Quantity per assembly = 2

Component 2

Purchase cost = $2.00

Quantity per assembly = 1

If a production lot of 200 assembly Gs is produced for safety stock, the dollar value of the addition to assembly Gs inventory is:

A. $400

B. $500

C. $2000

D. $2400

7. Which of the following is the correct formula for calculating inventory turns?

A. $$\frac{\text{Cost of Goods Sold}}{\text{Inventory}}$$

B. $$\frac{\text{Cost of Goods Sold}}{\text{Gross Profit Margin}}$$

C. $$\frac{\text{Sales}}{\text{Cost of Goods Sold}}$$

8. Which of the following is the correct formula for calculating Days' Sales Outstanding?

A. $$\frac{\text{Net Profit}}{\text{Stockholders' Equity}}$$

B. $$\frac{\text{Net Profit}}{\text{Assets}}$$

C. $$\frac{\text{Accounts Receivable} \times 365}{\text{Net Sales}}$$

D. $$\frac{\text{Current Assets}}{\text{Net Sales}}$$

9. Using the Balance Sheet and Income Statement below:

BALANCE SHEET
($ Million)

Assets		Liabilities	
Cash	20	Accounts Payable	20
A/R	10	Long-term debt	10
Inventory	10	Stockholders' equity	40
Machines/equip.	30		

INCOME STATEMENT

Net Sales	100
COGS	60
Gross Profit	40
Sales, General, & Admin.	30
Net Profit	10

I.   Calculate the ratio for Inventory Turns

II. Calculate the ratio for Return on Equity

III. Calculate the ratio for Days' Supply of Inventory

IV. Calculate the ratio for Days' Sales Outstanding

Answers: Exercise 1

- Cost of carrying the inventory, which includes the interest on money, cost of the space, and insurance. In many companies, this cost can be as much as 20% to 30% of the Balance Sheet's value of the inventory.

- Cost of people to receive, put away, issue out, and so on.

- Cost of people who count the inventory. (In the example of seven turns, with 52 days' supply of inventory, the same part will be counted a multitude of times.)

- The more inventory you have, the more difficult it is to maintain the accuracy of your inventory. The less accurate the inventory counts, the higher the probability of missing shipments.

- The more inventory that is sitting around, the higher the probability of quality problems occurring.

- The more inventory that is sitting around the higher the probability of obsolescence. This figure can easily be determined by looking up the inventory write-off account in the general ledger. Another way of estimating the potential inventory obsolescence is to do an "aging of the inventory." This aging report shows how long the inventory has been in the facility.

- The more inventory that is sitting around, the earlier capacity of machines and people is used. The earlier this capacity is used, the less flexibility there is to respond to such things as customer changes.

Answers: Exercise 2 - *Addendum*

The financial ramifications of the MRP Report (answers) are shown below:

Planning period = 6 periods

Level 0 Product F	Master Schedule Independent Demand	Week					
		1	2	3	4	5	6
	Gross Requirements	150	100	200	50	150	500
	Scheduled Receipts	250					
Lot size = 400	Projected On Hand = 250	350	250	50	0	250	150
Lead-time	Net Requirements					-150	-250
Offset = 3 weeks	Planned Order Receipts					400	400
	Planned Order Release		400	400			

	MRP Calculations for Product F	Week					
		1	2	3	4	5	6
Level 1	Gross Requirements		400	400			
Part G	Scheduled Receipts						
	On-hand = 250	250	200	150	150	150	150
Lot size = 350	Net Requirement(s)		-150	-200			
Lead-time	Planned Order Receipt		350	350			
Offset = 1 week	Planned Order Release	350	350				

	MRP Calculations for Product F	Week					
		1	2	3	4	5	6
Level 2	Gross Requirements	350	350				
Part J	Scheduled Receipts						
	On-hand = 350	0	250	250	250	250	250
Lot size = 600	Net Requirement(s)		-350				
Lead-time	Planned Order Receipt		600				
Offset = 1 week	Planned Order Release	600					

	MRP Calculations for Product F	Week					
		1	2	3	4	5	6
Level 3	Gross Requirements	600					
Part 10	Scheduled Receipts		1000				
	On-hand = 750	150	1150	1150	1150	1150	1150
Lot size = 1000	Net Requirement(s)						
Lead-time	Planned Order Receipt						
Offset = 6 weeks	Planned Order Release						

The 1000 units were released in a prior planning period.

Answers: Exercise 3

The impacts are:

Financial (Profitability) *1) ROA & ROI go down 2) Margins are reduced 3) Inventory turn go down 4) Revenue goes down 5) Cost goes up 6) Premium & Expediting charges increase over-time for part assembly*

Customer Satisfaction *1) Missed deliveries 2) Field failures—RMAS 3) Turn-key vs. assigned 4) Negative impact on customer satisfaction*

Productivity *1) Rework/scrap goes up 2) Utilization goes down 3) Capacity constantly occurs 4) Through-put goes down 5) Negative impact on employee moral*

Inventory *1) WIP builds 2) Inventory goes up*

Lead-time *1) Goes up*

It should be obvious now why bills of material, routings, and lead-time must be 100% accurate as soon as possible.

Consider a situation where each of four levels is in the bill of material is 99% accurate. The overall level of accuracy of the BOM would be 99 x 99 x 99 x 99 or only 96% accurate—not good enough.

Answers: Exercise 4

Your chart should look like this.

KEY FINANCIAL RATIOS

Name	Method of Calculation	Current Year		Prior Year	
Liquidity Current Ratio	Current Assets / Current Liabilities	$\frac{1471}{541}$	= 2.72	$\frac{1140}{354}$	= 3.22
Quick Ratio	Cash Through Receivables / Current Liabilities	$\frac{225+257+416=898}{543}$	= 1.65	$\frac{228+181+339=748}{354}$	= 2.11
Day's Sales Outstanding (DSO)	Receivables x 365 / Net Sales	$\frac{416 \times 365}{3694}$	= 41.11	$\frac{339 \times 365}{2817}$	= 43.92
Inventory Turnover	Cost of Goods Sold / Inventory	$\frac{3266}{494}$	= 6.61	$\frac{2534}{368}$	= 6.89
Days' Supply of Inventory	365 Days / Inventory Turns	$\frac{365}{6.61}$	= 55.22	$\frac{365}{6.89}$	= 52.98
Days' Payables Outstanding	Payables x 365 / Cost of Goods Sold	$\frac{416 \times 365}{3266}$	= 46.49	$\frac{294 \times 365}{2534}$	= 42.35
Leverage Debt-to-Equity	Total Liabilities / Stockholders' Equity	$\frac{929}{921}$	= 1.01	$\frac{745}{701}$	= 1.06
Profitability Return on Equity	Net Income Before Taxes / Stockholders' Equity	$\frac{238}{921}$	= .26	$\frac{174}{701}$	= .25
Return on Assets	Net Income Before Taxes / Total Assets	$\frac{238}{1850}$	= .13	$\frac{174}{1446}$	= .12

Answers: Exercise 5

PART 1:

Description of Impact	Current year	Inventory Reduction	
		50% Reduction	90% Reduction
Inventory Turns	6.61	13.2	66
Days' Supply of Inventory	55.2	27.2	5.5
Net Income Before Taxes	$238	↑ $74 to $312	↑ $134 to $472
Return on Assets Before Taxes	.13	$\frac{312}{1850} = .17$	$\frac{472}{1850} = .26$
Reduction in Lead-Times	N/A	↓ 50%	↓ 90%

PART II:

The impact on the net income would be:

Description of Impact	Current year	50% Reduction	90% Reduction
Inventory	$494	$247	$445
Carrying Cost = 30%		30%	30%
Impact on Net Income Before Taxes		$74	$134

The impact on other areas would include:

- **Direct Labor:** *1) Would not be committed to inventory too early 2) Could be used in other areas that are over-capacity 3) More flexibility to respond to customer changes*

- **Quality:** *1) Would potentially improve because smaller lot sizes would reduce the amount of inventory that would be subject to defects if they did happen*

- **Space and the related occupancy costs:** *1) Would decrease because the inventory would not be built before it was needed and materials would not be bought before required*

- **Indirect Labor:** *1) Would reduce the use of very expensive people attending shortages meetings that error probably caused.*

Answers: Review

Following are the answers for the Review Questions.

1. A

2. A

3. B

4. D

5. E

6. D

7. A

8. C

9. I. $60 \div 10 = 6$

   II. $10 \div 40 = .25$

   III. $365 \div 6 = 60.8$

   IV. $10 \times 365 \div 100 = 36.5$

CHAPTER

V

THREE
CASE STUDIES

LEARNING OBJECTIVES

After completing this chapter, you will be able to:

- Explain lessons learned when the forecast, Master Schedule, and Bills of Material are not properly managed

- Explain lessons learned from not properly clarifying terms and conditions of a contract and the related financial impact

- Explain lessons learned from not qualifying a supplier from a financial standpoint

CASE STUDY I: WHAT WE HAVE LEARNED

In this chapter, a series of events have taken place and are presented in a case study format. As the assistant change agent to the Asset Manager, you will be asked to review each event.

The case study is broken down into three parts.

PART I: Deals with the following Balance Sheet items: Cash, Accounts Receivable, Inventory and Machines; and the Income Statement items: Net Sales, Cost of Goods Sold and Profit or Loss.

PART 2: Deals with contract terms and conditions, and with the financials of a supplier of a unique part.

PART 3: Involves putting together a presentation of lessons learned throughout this book.

The Title of Your Presentation

What We Have Learned from Our Past

and

How We Are Going to Prevent These Mistakes in the Future!

In the case study you will be dealing with two products, Hawk-Eye—the existing, very successful product, and Eagle-Eye, the new product that was intended to replace the Hawk-Eye.

CURRENT (FIRST) MEETING

As you entered, the Master Scheduling Meeting was just beginning. In attendance were the Asset Manager, as well as C. Countemright (C²)—Director of Finance; F. Fish—Director of Marketing; E.C. Oops—the newly appointed Director of Engineering; E.O. Inventory—Director of Manufacturing; and F. Forecaster (F²)—the Master Scheduler. The General Manager, B. Burnemout (B.B.), was not present. B.B. rarely, if ever, attended these meetings. B.B.'s philosophy was "This was a manufacturing meeting, and they are responsible for the inventory and meeting schedule."

F² introduced Fish as the first presenter. Fish was really excited about the potential of the Eagle-Eye System. However, Fish wanted to first address the Hawk-Eye product forecast. The Hawk-Eye forecast was slowing down, but was still close to target. The current thinking was that customers for the Hawk-Eye had needs that must be met in the short term and could not wait for the Eagle-Eye product.

The Hawk-Eye forecast was utilizing almost all of the assigned capacity of the bottleneck work center. The Eagle-Eye product was going to use this same bottleneck work center and had been assigned what was considered adequate capacity.

It was hoped that inventory for the Hawk-Eye was substantial enough to handle current demand and field service requests. In fact E.O. had told the purchasing department to order more parts for inventory, just in case.

Fish had given the sales force a preview of the new system, with an explicit promise of not letting customers know about it, with the exception of perhaps a "few" key customers. Fish said, "We'll rely on the common sense of the salespeople in this matter." Fish also mentioned in passing that a vice president of manufacturing of a large customer had recently canceled an order for five Hawk-Eye Systems. This translated to several million dollars, but that could easily be offset with all the new business from the Eagle-Eye System.

E.C. spoke next. Prior to the promotion, E.C. had worked on a customer support team. Rumor had it that E.C. had not dotted the "i's" and crossed the "t's" and, as a result, had created an "opportunity" for the remaining members of the customer satisfaction team. The Asset Manager asked you to make a note of this and look into this situation later on.

E.C. was very enthusiastic and felt that Fish's forecast was conservative and warned manufacturing to be ready. E.C. recommended that the sales forecast be increased.

E.C. went on to say that unlike prior directors, who repeatedly communicated schedules that showed just three more months, things would now be different. E.C. then proceeded to show an updated schedule that showed the completion date for the end of the current quarter.

MEETING THE PRODUCTION SCHEDULE

E.C. said that in order to meet this schedule, the following three recommendations would have to be implemented immediately.

1. The New Product Introduction Process, while exactly what the company needed, might have to be circumvented on "rare" occasions.
2. Inventory control for the new product needed to be transferred to manufacturing. All inventory should become an asset under manufacturing, rather than under engineering.
3. Manufacturing should assume responsibility for obtaining material.

Remembering that E.C. had boasted on more than one occasion about being single-handedly responsible for 80% of all Engineering Change Orders (ECOs) on the Hawk-Eye product, the Manufacturing Manager raised concern about the completeness of the Bill of Material. E.C.'s reply was "no problem," the BOM was in great shape, with only one or two parts yet to be specified, and added that there were some loose ends to tie up on a part that was unique. But he quickly added it was being resolved and that marketing should proceed with pricing the product.

Based on E.C.'s presentation, another recommendation was made.

4. The BOM was to be transferred to manufacturing, and the purchasing department should finish tying up the loose ends with the supplier of the unique part. It was further noted that this software supplier was having a little *trouble* making the software Y2K compliant.

B.B. enters the room.

At this point, the level of enthusiasm was reaching a crescendo; visions of stock options were dancing in everyone's head. "Let's put the darn thing (Eagle-Eye) on the Master Schedule," B.B. suggested. "We need to ramp up production and quickly ship products, this takes precedence over all other issues," B.B. explained. B.B. further stated all four of the recommendations are to be implemented. "Any Questions?"

E.O., not wanting to be accused of not being a team player agreed, even though E.O. wondered how they would find enough capacity? E.O. thought silently, "I hope this demand pull stuff works."

The meeting was adjourned with assurance from marketing, manufacturing, and engineering that everything was in good shape, and the Asset Manager should worry only about the numbers.

As the Manufacturing Manager passed, a slouch of shoulders and a glazed look in the eyes could be noted.

Summary of Decisions (So Far)

_____

_____

_____

_____

_____

_____

FOLLOW-UP MEETING

E.C. enthusiastically brought the meeting to order. "I have a number of things to update everyone on, so let's get started," E.C. said. "To begin with, I have just been promoted to Senior Director of Engineering, so a Rapid Implementation Plan (RIP) will need to be established with a reassignment of tasks from our last meeting. It's been determined that perhaps you were a little too ambitious with your assessment of what could be accomplished. Since I saw this coming, I took it upon myself to brief the executives of the grave situation you find yourselves in. They agreed with my proposal, as well as my promotion. So team, let's get started!"

Fish was first to speak. "It seems we have had a bit of a turndown in business." Fish said, "The downturn in the Far East seems to have had impacted our business…more than expected."

Fish went on to say that the Master Schedule was probably unrealistic during the Eagle-Eye development and F^2 was still forecasting an unrealistic build schedule (F^2 was told by the manufacturing manager to continue with the existing forecast until marketing said to do otherwise. Let them take the heat, E.O. had said.) Fish went on to say that F^2 should fix the forecast immediately by decreasing last year's net sales by 20%, which translates to about $100 million.

Fish next reported that Eagle-Eye had been announced to select customers during its development, which resulted in the "Osborne Effect": These customers held off buying Hawk-Eye series equipment, waiting for the introduction of the new Eagle-Eye.

Fish next said that customers were requesting late changes in configuration for the new product. It was not clearly understood how long it would take to make these configuration changes, how much it would cost, or the impact this would cause in the ability to meet schedules and deliver parts.

The Hawk-Eye refurb business was taking key work-center capacity that could have been used to build Eagle-Eye machines.

MORE BAD NEWS

Fish continued in a quavering voice:

Capacity requirements for building the Eagle-Eye were not fully understood.

Inventory was continuing to build up and shipments were not being made.

The problem with the software supplier of Y2K had pushed the delivery date out another three months. The Eagle-Eye units that had been shipped were operating on the old Y99 software.

In the meantime, customers were getting nervous. As of this date, five customers representing more than $100 million in sales had already canceled their orders, returned the Eagle-Eye product, and went to the competition.

Five other customers, totaling $150 million in shipped products, had agreed to continue using the Y99 software for six more months, if the company agreed to extend the A/R for six months, absorb any maintenance expenses ($100,000 so far), and start the warranty when and if the Y2K software was delivered. If they were not delivered in the next six months, all machines could be returned and the money refunded. These machines would then be reclassified as used equipment.

Additionally, many customers changed their minds and decided to go with the good ole' reliable Hawk-Eye, however, because increases on these orders had not been forecasted, the following events were starting to take place.

- Partially built Eagle-Eye machines were being disassembled to meet the demand for the Hawk-Eye. Quality problems were starting to show up.
- Inventory of key parts for the Hawk-Eye were in short supply. Premium and expedite fees were being incurred. (Approximately $100,000).

Because of the problems with Eagle-Eye and the increase in demand for Hawk-Eye, a decision was made to redesign Hawk-Eye to meet customer requests. This impacted the inventory of parts for Hawk-Eyes even more since they had been projected to decrease. It also impacted the capacity of the bottleneck work center.

E.O. Speaks

Next, E.O. addressed the group. E.O.'s group had just finished an analysis of the inventory, which had been transferred from engineering. E.O. also had information on the BOM that E.C. had indicated was almost complete. Following are the results.

- $20 million in inventory had been shifted to manufacturing, based on E.C.'s suggestion, which contained $13 million of obsolete material that had not been reserved. The auditor insisted that the entire amount be written off prior to the current year end.
- The MRP system assumed the lead-time to build an Eagle-Eye system required only 11 weeks, In fact, it was taking 22 weeks, with 50% of the purchase and manufacturing orders past due.
- Dates and material receipts diverged from the actual schedule required to execute planned shipments. The material plan had used the lead-time, input by engineering, without asking purchasing. Purchasing had not questioned them when these parts transferred to manufacturing.

- The lead-times were reset allowing for 22 weeks of build time. This event, coupled with missed shipment dates, led to the following results:
  - This increase in cycle time was more realistic, it allowed for better planning, however it meant that inventory turns declined drastically.
  - Although build times were more realistic, to the extent the Master Schedule was over-committed, excess inventory would take an additional three months to work off.

- Inventory was continuing to build and shipments were not being made for the following reasons:
  - The level of WIP increased by another $30 million because of the inability to ship Eagle-Eye products as forecasted, and this reduction was not communicated to purchasing, so the suppliers would stop shipping parts.
  - Another $10 million sat in containers under tents because of inadequate warehouse space.
  - The accounting entries had not been made.

- Capacity requirements for building the Eagle-Eye were not fully understood. Customers were requesting late changes in configuration for products. No one knew how long it would take to make these configuration changes, what it would cost, or if it would impact the ability to meet schedules and deliver parts. The costs and schedule slippage needed to be estimated.

- Hawk-Eye was taking work center capacity that could have been used to build Eagle-Eye.

- A partial BOM was presented. Manufacturing was now responsible for obtaining material, but had only about 80% of the information necessary to do this. Not all parts had been identified. Prior to the transfer of inventory to manufacturing, engineers had been focused on the base technology and had not been concerned with these other parts, so the BOM was incomplete. Part # 1 was missing completely and the supplier had not completed the new part #3.

- During the field testing of Eagle-Eye, a major defect had been discovered, which caused a hazardous situation. ECOs were being written, which by one estimate would result in $50 million worth of obsolete parts. Since the field had already been stocked with replacement parts, there was potential impact here as well. The problem was made even more difficult because there was no one common system that tracked field inventory on the seven field service locations throughout the world.

EXERCISE 1: CASE STUDY I

In this exercise you are asked to recap the results of the events described in the prior pages. Use the space provided below. See page 132 for the answers.

What should be done to resolve this case (this should be an open-discussion forum).

What are the lessons learned?

_____

_____

_____

_____

_____

What are the potential financial impacts?

_____

_____

_____

_____

_____

What are the dollar impacts?

_____

_____

_____

_____

_____

_____

_____

CASE STUDY II: CONTRACT TERMS AND CONDITIONS

In the next part of the case study, we will look at a situation involving contract terms and conditions.

Fish was an ambitious person. Fish had sold the pre-released Eagle-Eye II to a customer. Fish and E.C. had co-led a "Customer Satisfaction Team" that had worked very hard at making this sale successful. During the final throws of the negotiation, Fish had left the final dotting of the "i's" and crossing of the "t's" to E.C. Apparently, E.C. had not done the job and now Fish had to explain to that "Corporate Bean Counter"—Asset Manager—what had been learned and why it was not going to happen in the future. Fish wondered where E.C. was, why E.C. wasn't here to take some of the heat. Fortunately, Fish had been able to delegate most of this to the Legal Beagles. "Let them figure this out."

The Asset Manager arrived at this point with Chris C. Grissem—Corporate Lawyer who was to summarize findings to Fish, the Asset Manager, and E.C.—if he ever showed up. "Boy, is this the stuff fiction is made of," thought Fish as the presentation started.

Background

Chris C. Grissem started out by giving the following background:

"Customer Terms and Conditions are the written contractual arrangements between the company and its customers. In a perfect world, clearly specified terms and conditions define precisely what, when, and how we will deliver to avoid delivery delays and disputes with the customer. In the absence of well-specified terms and conditions, problems can arise leading to expensive delays in delivery of products and payment for those products.

A critical part of new business and ongoing account maintenance is the customer contract. The contract is the agreement between the company and a customer in areas including (but not limited to) the scope of work, product forecasts, material procurement, purchase orders and pricing reviews, delivery, payment terms, engineering changes, inventory management, confidentiality, warranty, and termination. The initial contract negotiation is typically led by Sales. Most contracts use Standard Manufacturing Agreements as a basis for negotiation. The negotiation process will proceed by adding or deleting items from the standard contract until mutual agreement is reached, or by using the supplier's standard or modified vendor contract.

A thorough understanding of the agreements between the company and a customer is essential.

Chris C. Grissem went on to recap the events of the current customer situation.

Additionally, communication between departments is key. Marketing, manufacturing, engineering and finance all must know exactly what is expected. The more precise a company's terms and conditions are, the less likely it is that problems will occur.

Facts of the Situation

- Several months ago, a customer from the Far East ordered one Eagle-Eye inspection system, including the operating software package Y2K, scheduled for release six months from the order date, for their manufacturing plant in Taiwan. The terms and conditions for this sale stipulated that the customer would pay 80% thirty days after shipment, and 20% thirty days after final acceptance. Payments were secured by a letter of credit from the Bank of Taipei. Warranty is scheduled to begin at the time of final acceptance.

- Several months ago, the machine was tentatively accepted by the customer in our plant running on software release Y99 with the assumption that Y2K would be available within a reasonable period of time.

- The machine was then installed successfully in the customer's plant in Taipei; however, software release Y2K has been delayed for several months. The company invoiced 80% of the cost of the hardware at this time, and planned to invoice for the final 20% when the new software was satisfactorily installed.

- The customer still wanted software release Y2K, but decided to put the equipment into production at 80% of expected performance with release Y99. The customer refused final acceptance of the machines pending release Y2K.

- When the bank received the invoice from the company for the partial payment, it informed the company that it would not be paid since the letter of credit didn't allow for partial payments, and that release Y2K had not been shipped.

- After several weeks of operation, the equipment needed periodic maintenance, however, the warranty had not begun. The company provided the service.

- It will cost several thousand dollars to amend the letter of credit, and after several weeks of discussion about who will pay for the amendment, the company decides to wait until the software is finished and installed before seeking payment from the bank.

- A few days ago, you learned that the software will be delayed again. The decision was again made to wait until the software was completed to seek payment from the bank.

- A few days ago, the letter of credit with the Bank of Taipei expired turning the customer into an open account, in other words, the company has, in effect, extended credit to the customer for the value of the system.

- The company's ongoing service costs continue to mount.

EXERCISE 1: CASE STUDY II

In this exercise you are asked to recap the results of the events described in the prior pages. Use the space provided below. See page 134 for the answers.

What should be done to resolve this case (this should be an open-discussion forum).

What are the lessons learned?

_____

_____

_____

_____

_____

_____

_____

What are the potential financial impacts?

_____

_____

_____

_____

_____

_____

_____

_____

_____

_____

CASE STUDY III: SUPPLIER WITH BAD FINANCIALS

Titanic Software Systems

The Asset Manager reviewed the presentation that the "star" engineer, E.C. Oops, now Senior Director of Engineering, had presented to the Purchasing Department, which now preferred to be called Supply-Chain Management. E.C. had been one of four engineers on the project, and often boasted about single-handedly accounting for 80% of all Engineering Change Orders (ECOs).

Over a year had been spent attempting to qualify a manufacturer to design the software. (The one E.C. had mentioned during the last meeting.) It seems this supplier was now in a bit of financial trouble.

The supplier was now asking for cash in advance for work left to complete. It seems the supplier had been impacted by the recession in the Far East.

In addition to the financial problems the company was encountering, their chief design engineer had succumbed to a heart-attack—and in a hospital bed—was being hampered in his ability to produce code. However, the president of the company had written a letter assuring that all possible steps were being taken. The engineer had just been given a faster lap-top. Finally, every effort was being taken to find additional engineering help. However, since engineers seldom used a formalized New Product Introduction Process, the suppliers would have to start from scratch. The software due-date would have to be pushed out again.

As the Asset Manager reviewed the supplier's financials that E.C. had put together for Titanic Software Systems, it seems E.C. had done some homework.

E.C. and the team had found the supplier of the state-of-the-art software, Y2K, for the Eagle-Eye inspection equipment. E.C. indicated that even though the software hadn't been tested, the Department of Defense had just approved the sales of the software to a Middle-Eastern company, so it must be okay to use. E.C. had also brought back the financial statements that are shown on the next two pages.

In the following exercise, the Asset Manager has given you two sets of financial statements. The first exhibit is the one E.C. and the team used to evaluate the supplier during the selection process (financial statement marked "Prior Year"). The second set was a set provided per the Asset Manager's request (financial statement marked "Current Year").

You are to perform a ratio analysis and then make recommendations to resolve this situation with Titanic Software Systems.

Titanic Software Systems
PRIOR YEAR'S BALANCE SHEET
($Million)

	Prior Year		Prior Year
Current Assets		**Current Liabilities**	
Cash	80	Accounts Payable	100
Accts. Receivable	160	Short-term debt	120
Inventories		**Total Current Liabilities**	**220**
Raw materials	60		
Work-in-process	60	**Long-Term Liabilities**	
Finished goods	90	Long-term debt	315
Total inventories	210	**TOTAL LIABILITIES**	**535**
Total Current Assets	**450**		
		Shareholders' Equity	
Property, Plant and Equipment		Common stock	53
Land	45	Accumulated retained earnings	**487**
Buildings	220		
Machinery, equip., tools	535		
Total Prop., Plant Equip.	**800**	**Total Shareholders' Equity**	**540**
Less accum. Depreciation	(175)		
Net Property, Plant, Equip.	**625**		
TOTAL ASSETS	**1,075**	**Total Liabilities and Shareholders' Equity**	**1,075**

Titanic Software Systems
INCOME STATEMENT
($Million)

	Prior Year
Net Sales (Revenue)	**2,000**
Cost of Sales and Operating Expenses	
Cost of goods sold	1,300
Gross profit	700
Sales, general, and administrative expenses	320
Operating profit	380
Other Income (expenses)	
Interest expense	(60)
Net Income Before Taxes	320
Provision for Federal Income Taxes	(140)
Net Income	180

Titanic Software Systems
UPDATED BALANCE SHEET
($Million)

	Updated		Updated
Current Assets		**Current Liabilities**	
Cash	100	Accounts Payable	300
Accts. Receivable	200	Short-term debt	400
Inventories		**Total Current Liabilities**	**700**
Raw materials	100		
Work-in-process	400	**Long-Term Liabilities**	
Finished goods	215	Long-term debt	440
Total inventories	715	**TOTAL LIABILITIES**	**1,440**
Total Current Assets	**1,015**		
		Shareholders' Equity	
		Common stock	55
Property, Plant and Equipment		Accumulated retained earnings	**565**
Land	50		
Buildings	340		
Machinery, equip., tools	610		
Total Prop., Plant Equip.	**1,000**	**Total Shareholders' Equity**	**620**
Less accum. Depreciation	(255)		
Net Property, Plant, Equip.	**745**		
TOTAL ASSETS	**1,760**	**Total Liabilities and Shareholders' Equity**	**1,760**

Titanic Software Systems
INCOME STATEMENT
($Million)

	Updated
Net Sales (Revenue)	**1,600**
Cost of Goods Sold and Operating Expenses	
Cost of goods sold	900
Gross profit	700
Sales, general, and administrative expenses	240
Operating profit	460
Other Income (expenses)	
Interest expenses	(20)
Net Income Before Taxes	440
Provision for Federal Income Taxes	(200)
Net Income	**240**

EXERCISE 1: CASE STUDY III

Key Financial Ratios

Using the Financial Statements, calculate the following ratios (round all decimals back two places). See page 135 for the answers.

Name	Method of Calculation	Initial	Updated
Liquidity Current Ratio	$$\frac{\text{Current Assets}}{\text{Current Liabilities}}$$		
Quick Ratio	$$\frac{\text{Cash Through Receivables}}{\text{Current Liabilities}}$$		
Days Sales Outstanding (DSO)	$$\frac{\text{Receivables} \times 365}{\text{Net Sales}}$$		
Inventory Turnover (Turns)	$$\frac{\text{Cost of Goods Sold}}{\text{Inventory}}$$		
Days' Supply of Inventory	$$\frac{365 \text{ Days}}{\text{Inventory Turns}}$$		
Days' Payables Outstanding	$$\frac{\text{Payables} \times 365}{\text{Cost of Goods Sold}}$$		
Leverage Debt-to-Equity	$$\frac{\text{Total Liabilities}}{\text{Stockholders' Equity}}$$		
Profitability Return on Equity	$$\frac{\text{Net Income Before Taxes}}{\text{Stockholders' Equity}}$$		
Return on Assets	$$\frac{\text{Net Income Before Taxes}}{\text{Total Assets}}$$		

Now update the supply chain cash-to-cash worksheet on page 69.

EXERCISE 2: CASE STUDY III

After making a careful analysis of the previous supporting financial statements, answer the following questions. See page 136 for the answers.

What should be done to resolve this case (this should be an open-discussion forum)?

What are the lessons learned?

_____

_____

_____

_____

_____

_____

_____

_____

What are the potential financial impacts?

_____

_____

_____

_____

_____

_____

_____

_____

Answers: Case Study I

Lessons Learned

- Schedules should be realistic, with the least negative impact on inventory.
- Product obsolescence plans should be developed and implemented.
- The transfer from engineering to manufacturing should be well organized to minimize inventory risks. Communication between these two areas is vital.
- Manufacturing should not Master Schedule an incomplete, untested product.
- Factor in critical path lead-times when changing Master Schedule completion dates.
- Product announcements should not be made to customers prematurely.
- The New Product Introduction process should be followed more closely, enhancing communication among all areas working on a project. Include excess inventory and product obsolescence plans in the New Product Introduction process.
- Pay close attention to targeted levels of inventory turns. If this target is not achieved, search out and resolve causes immediately.
- Accurate forecasts are important for products with a long lead-time and many options.
- Watch targeted levels of inventory turns. If target isn't achieved, find and resolve the cause(s).
- Define clear boundaries for long-term contracts with outside vendors (length contract, provisions for sell-back, and so on).
- Manufacturing needs to take the inputs from the product-responsible group, incorporate the correct number of units in the Master Schedule, and then execute the MRP in a timely (immediate) and disciplined manner. They should *not* be deciding how many units to build. The Master Schedule must be signed off at the end of the monthly Master Schedule meeting.
- Accurate sales forecasting and a well-executed MRP are essential to inventory management.
- Revise and review regularly the Master Schedule so demand and supply can be accurately accounted for.
- Eliminate excess safety stock.
- Buy parts when a product is ordered, rather than buying parts based on anticipated sales.
- Redesign product for manufacturability before ordering parts. Ensure manufacturability before ordering parts. Ensure manufacturability before ordering parts for future products.
- Develop an overall inventory model to track inventory of all products.
- Send back excess inventory where possible.
- Provide additional training for managers.
- Follow the NPI process more closely, including plans for product obsolescence.
- Increase communication and control from top management.
- Manufacturing should not Master Schedule an incomplete, untested product.
- Factor in critical path lead-times when changing Master Schedule completion dates.
- Develop an overall strategy for inventory management.
- Develop networking among countries, so that all inventory is visible and accounted for.
- Reduce repair cycle times and backlog; scrap old inventory not used for repairs.
- Move repair of old parts out of manufacturing, as repair conflicts with manufacturing.

- Significantly reduce the number of inventory sites, and coordinate inventory management among those sites.
- Develop a process to manage ECOs.

Potential Financial Impacts

- Consider the costs incurred by configuration changes, the impact of configuration changes on the capacity to plan, and ability to meet commitments to customers.
- Upside potential must be managed during product transitions.
- Engineering should buy materials only for engineering. These materials should be treated as a project expense, rather than being inventoried. These materials should be identified and any obsolete material reserved prior to transferring to manufacturing.
- Manufacturing should buy inventory for production.
- Sales forecasts should be realistic, rather than overly optimistic; repeated inaccuracies should be factored into the credibility of future forecasts for purposes of driving the Master Schedule.
- After considering inputs from all sources and evaluating the business and economic climate, the general manager needs to make the decision as to the build plan even when it conflicts with the marketing group and corporate forecasts/targets (easier said then done). *The general manager is the ultimate authority in deciding what manufacturing should build.*
- The Director of Finance should be ensuring that the number of units agreed to at the Master Schedule meeting is incorporated into the next MRP. In other words, the basic account equation must match in dollars and units.
- Reduce cost of products to increase sales.

Dollar Impact

- Reduction in sales forecast by 20% = $100,000,000
- $150 million if new product not delivered in six months
- Cancellation of $100,000,000 in sales contracts
- Maintenance expenses total $100,000
- Premium and Expedite fees of $100,000 are incurred
- Obsolete inventory now totals $13,000,000
- There is $10,000,000 in never-recorded inventory

Answers: Case Study II

Lessons Learned

Unclear terms and conditions can lead to delays in the company receiving payment for its products. As we've seen, this can be extremely costly. Customer terms have to be worked out in advance in precise detail. They must match exactly what you say you'll do. It is vital that both the customer's and the company's expectations are clearly set forth in writing. The company and the customer must agree on such issues as:

- What will be delivered and when, the shipping terms, and who pays taxes
- How it will be configured—technical specifications
- Payment terms, including whether payments will be secured or unsecured, and credit limits
- What constitutes acceptance—both at the factory and at the customer's site
- Whether or not to take orders for products that are not completely developed
- If the customer's warranty will begin before final acceptance
- If the bank will pay even though the letter of credit expires
- If the client can be billed for payment based on the current percent usability of the systems
- Whether to include a "no later than" payment clause in all letters of credit to ensure that they don't expire
- Who bears the risk of loss, and who pays the insurance
- Terms for settling disputes

Additionally, the following items are vitally important

- General Management should be at meetings
- Schedules and forecasts need to be realistic
- Don't transfer incomplete BOMs from NPI to production

Potential Financial Impacts

- Missed customer shipments, which impacts related sales and Accounts Receivable
- Possible negative impact on cash flow
- Days' sales outstanding goes up
- Lead-times might increase
- ROA might go down

Answers: Exercise 1: Case Study III

Key Financial Ratios

(round all decimals back two places)

Name	Method of Calculation	ANSWERS Prior Period	Updated
Liquidity Current Ratio	$\dfrac{\text{Current Assets}}{\text{Current Liabilities}}$	$\dfrac{450}{220}$ = 2.05	$\dfrac{1015}{700}$ = 1.45
Quick Ratio	$\dfrac{\text{Cash Through Receivables}}{\text{Current Liabilities}}$	$\dfrac{80+160=240}{220}$ = 1.09	$\dfrac{100+200}{700}$ = .43
Days Sales Outstanding (DSO)	$\dfrac{\text{Receivables} \times 365}{\text{Net Sales}}$	$\dfrac{160\times365=58400}{2000}$ = 29.2	$\dfrac{200\times365=73000}{1600}$ = 45.6
Inventory Turnover (Turns)	$\dfrac{\text{Cost of Goods Sold}}{\text{Inventory}}$	$\dfrac{1300}{210}$ = 6.19	$\dfrac{900}{715}$ = 1.26
Days' Supply of Inventory	$\dfrac{365 \text{ Days}}{\text{Inventory Turns}}$	$\dfrac{365}{6.19}$ = 58.97	$\dfrac{365}{1.26}$ = 289.67
Days' Payables Outstanding	$\dfrac{\text{Payables} \times 365}{\text{Cost of Goods Sold}}$	$\dfrac{100\times365=36500}{1300}$ = 28.08	$\dfrac{300\times365=109550}{900}$ = 121.67
Leverage Debt-to-Equity	$\dfrac{\text{Total Liabilities}}{\text{Stockholders' Equity}}$	$\dfrac{535}{540}$ = .99	$\dfrac{1440}{620}$ = 2.32
Profitability Return on Equity	$\dfrac{\text{Net Income Before Taxes}}{\text{Stockholders' Equity}}$	$\dfrac{320}{540}$ = .59	$\dfrac{440}{620}$ = .71
Return on Assets	$\dfrac{\text{Net Income Before Taxes}}{\text{Total Assets}}$	$\dfrac{320}{1075}$ = .30	$\dfrac{440}{1760}$ = .25

Answers: Exercise 2: Case Study III

Lessons Learned

Consider the following information as you review the financial stability and suitability of another company's financial situation.

- Watch for slow-paying customers or heavy dependence on one slow-paying customer. Check the days' sales outstanding (DSO) ratio.
- Is the company rapidly expanding to meet customer demands?
- Do they have a heavy investment requirement in new technology?
- Is there evidence of insufficient knowledge of its costs and, as a result, inappropriate pricing?
- Are there poor internal cost controls?
- Did they stop taking advantage of discounts for early payment?
- Have they had problems making delivery schedules?
- Do they factor their receivables (for example, do they sell them to a bank or finance company)?
- Do they request early payment from customers?
- Is there inventory that appears to be moving slowly? (Check the inventory turnover ratio and, if possible, the inventory aging.)
- Do they have low current and acid-test ratios?
- Is there a history of difficulties meeting commitments to its lenders? (Check the debt-to-equity and debt-service ratios. Also check the banking statements on the Dun & Bradstreet to see if the bank indicates any problems.)

In addition, the following are important:

- A competitive analysis of two years' financials should always be done.
- In a start-up company, these financials should reviewed quarterly.
- A detailed review of the organization should be made, including the software organization.

Potential Financial Impact

- Missed shipments and subsequent loss of sales and Accounts Receivable
- Might have to invest in the supplier to keep them solvent
- Inventory turns might go down
- Days' supple of inventory might go up
- Lead-times might increase
- ROA might go down

CHAPTER

VI

FINAL PRESENTATION

LEARNING OBJECTIVES

Now that you have completed this book, you should be able to:

- Complete the Final Presentation

PUTTING IT ALL TOGETHER

Now it is time for you to pull together all the lessons learned into a final presentation. Based on one of your key objectives (customer, team, department) for the coming year, put together a presentation incorporating what you have learned.

Presentation Items

- Key competitive issues identified in the first chapter
- A problem statement
- Solutions, with a time estimate to complete it and with financial benefits to your company, and if appropriate, for the customer and the supplier
- Lessons learned—These should relate to not only your specific area, but include lessons learned that impact the company in general

In Class or On Your Own

If you are doing this presentation in the classroom, check with your instructor as to how much detail the presentation should include. Because situations vary so much from student to student, it is strongly suggested that this final presentation be done on separate sheets of paper. If you are doing this on your own, you still might want to work on separate sheets of paper so that you won't feel limited by the amount of space given here. Realize also that the presentation will vary depending on whether you are in manufacturing, finance, sales, R&D, program management, and so on.

Item #1   Key Competitive Issues

_____

_____

_____

_____

_____

_____

_____

_____

_____

_____

Item #2 *Lessons Learned from This Book/Course*

- Your specific area
- Company in general

_____

_____

_____

_____

_____

_____

_____

Item #3 *Problem Statement*

_____

_____

_____

_____

_____

_____

_____

_____

_____

Item #4   **Financial Benefits**

_____

_____

_____

_____

_____

_____

Item #5   **Solutions**

_____

_____

_____

_____

_____

_____

Item #6   **Timeline/Steps to Be Taken**

(Include time estimates of when you expect to complete the implementation of the recommended solution)

_____

_____

_____

_____

_____

Congratulations! Now test your understanding of the material you have covered in this book. Turn to page 146 and take the post-test.

THE END

Congratulations on completing this book. I hope you found that your time was well spent and that you have added to your skills portfolio.

I also hope this book contributed to the integration of key manufacturing concepts and their corresponding financial impact.

I firmly believe that as we go forward in the future, the integration of knowledge horizontally across the supply chain, as well as vertically within each component of the supply chain, will be essential.

As a result, I am currently working on the next two books in the Basics of Manufacturing series:

- *Basics of Supply Chain Collaboration*
- *Basics of Contract Manufacturing—A Global Approach*

See you there.

I would enjoy hearing from you, so I have attached the following feedback sheet, which can be forwarded to me by:

FAX:	408/973-1592
PHONE:	408/973-0309
E-MAIL:	CFME@aol.com

For additional information regarding in-house training, book purchases, or our free newsletter, visit our Web page at: www.CFME.com.

PRETEST

1. Most companies payment terms are:

      A. Net 15

      B. Net 25

      C. Net 30

      D. Net 40

2. Most companies collection terms are:

      A. Net 20

      B. Net 40

      C. Net 50

      D. None of the above

3. The formula for calculating inventory turns is:

      A. Revenue ÷ Cost of goods sold

      B. Last three months ending Inventory ÷ Cost of goods sold

      C. COGS ÷ Inventory

      D. None of the above

4. The formula for calculating days' sales outstanding is:

      A. COGS ÷ Total shipments

      B. COGS ÷ 90 days

      C. Future COGS ÷ Ending inventory

      D. COGS ÷ Future revenue

      E. Receivables x 365 ÷ Net sales

5. The formula for calculating Return on Assets is:

      A. Net Income ÷ Total assets

      B. Gross Profit ÷ Total assets

      C. Current Assets ÷ Total assets

6. The formula for calculating Return on Equity is:

      A. Last three months' profit after taxes x 4 Qtrs. ÷ Last 3 months average assets

      B. Net Income ÷ Stockholders' equity

      C. Ending Accounts Receivable ÷ Revenue

      D. None of the above

7. The gross profit margin on an account doing $10 million in annual sales and $1 million in profit is:

    A. .01%

    B. 1.0%

    C. 10%

    D. 20%

    E. None of the above

8. ROA can best improved by (circle all that apply):

    A. Increasing your inventory turns

    B. Improving kit drop performance

    C. Improving the accuracy of your forecast

    D. Charging the customer inventory carrying cost

    E. Reducing your DSO

9. Select one statement that is NOT true:

    A. A Parts represent 80% of the extended dollars and 20% of the part number

    B. B Parts represent 15% of the extended dollars and 50% of the part number

    C. C Parts represent 5% of the extended dollars and 50% of the part number

10. Safety stock

    A. Is used to satisfy upside flexibility

    B. Increases costs

    C. Requires management approval

    D. Is consistent with JIT principals

    E. A & B

    F. C & D

    G. A, B, & C

11. Lead-time refers to:

    A. The time it takes to receive material from a supplier

    B. The point from when a PO is received to when a customer receives their shipment

    C. The time period required from material procurement through shipment

    D. A & C

12. The parent component relationship in a Bill of Material (BOM) is needed to:

    A. Show the relationship to different levels of the BOM

    B. Set the lead-time for each step

    C. Provide an accurate quote

    D. All of the above

13. The formula for quick ratio is:

    A. Current assets ÷ Current liabilities

    B. Cash from Accounts Receivable ÷ Current liabilities

    C. A & B

    D. None of the above

14. Code 0 in a BOM refers to:

    A. The lowest level of the BOM

    B. The top or product level

    C. None of the above

15. In general terms, the difference between capacity and rated capacity is:

    A. There is no difference

    B. Rated capacity includes factor for utilization and efficiency

    C. Capacity includes programming, set-up time, efficiency, and so on

    D. All of the above

POST-TEST

Use the data below to answer the following questions.

	Month #3
Accounts Receivable	$ 2,500
Net Sales	$1,000
Inventory	$ 90
Fixed Assets	$ 750
COGS:	$ 900
Operating Expenses	$ 50
Other (Income) / Expense	$ 10
Tax Rate	40%

1. What is the DSO?
2. Calculate inventory turns.
3. How many DOS do you have?
4. Calculate:

   A. Gross Profit _____

   B. Operating Income _____

   C. Profit Below Taxes _____

   D. Profit After Taxes _____

   E. ROA _____

Use the data below to answer the following questions.

5. Your customer has asked you to provide a discount if they pay in 15 days, instead of in 30 days. What would the impact be on your ROA if the customer paid in 15 days without you granting a discount?
6. In order to achieve the same ROA as before, how much of a discount could you offer?

7. If the unit cost is $200, calculate the selling price of a unit that has an 18% margin (round to the nearest dollar).

    A. $244

    B. $236

    C. $263

    D. None of the above

8. If the unit cost is $200, calculate the selling price of a unit that has a mark-up of 18%.

    A. $263

    B. $236

    C. $254

    D. None of the above

9. In manufacturing companies, which calculation should be used for calculating selling price?

    A. Mark-up %

    B. Margin %

    C. Neither A nor B

    D. Both A and B

Answers: Pretest

1. C	9. C
2. D	10. G
3. C	11. D
4. D	12. A
5. B	13. B
6. C	14. B
7. E	15. B
8. A	

Answers: Post-Test

1. $2500 \div 1000 = 2.5$

2. $900 \div 90 = 10$

3. $365 \div 10 = 36.5$

4. Calculations are as follows:

      A. $1000 - 900 = 100$

      B. $1000 - 900 - 50 = 50$

      C. $50 - 10 = 40$

      D. $40 \times 40\% = 16; 40 - 16 = 24$

      E. $24 \div 2500 + 90 = .01$

5. $1200 \div 4000 = 30\%$ = current ROA, if the customer pays in 15 days instead of 30, receivables goes down 50% to 600.

   (Formula is: $1200 \div (600 + 1000 + 1800) = 1200 \div 3400 = 35.29$

6. To achieve the same ROA as before:

      $1200 \div 3400 = 30\%$

      $30\% \times 3400 = 1020$

      $1020 \div 1200 - 1.00 = 15$

7. A (Formula is: $200 \div (1 - .18) = 243.90$ or 244)

8. B ($200 \times 1.18 = 236$)

9. B

EVALUATION FORM

I. Clarity of the Content

1. Are there any contradictions in the book? ❏ Yes ❏ No

   If yes, please identify the page numbers and specifics below. _____

   _____

2. Is there any redundancy in the book? ❏ Yes ❏ No

   If yes, please identify the page numbers and specifics below. _____

   _____

3. Are there any major content areas missing that you feel should be added to this book? ❏ Yes ❏ No

   If yes, please list specifics below. _____

   _____

4. Are there any terms or definitions that need clarification? ❏ Yes ❏ No

   If yes, please list these terms below. _____

   _____

II. Questions and Case Studies

5. Are there any questions or case studies written in a way you could not understand? ❏ Yes ❏ No

   If yes, please note questions and page numbers below. _____

   _____

6. Are there any answers to questions or case studies you think are incorrect or incomplete? ❏ Yes ❏ No

   If yes, please note questions and page numbers below. _____

   _____

7. Are there any activities or exercises that should be considered for exclusion in the next revision of this book? ❏ Yes ❏ No _____

   _____

   _____

Please return completed form by mail to:

MAIL: CFME Press 1639 Daphne Drive, San Jose, CA 95129
FAX: (408) 973-1592